About the Book

This authoritative book is a new title in the *Observer's* series. It covers a wide range of tractors, implements drawn by tractors, and self-propelled machinery in use in agriculture, and for most kinds of terrain, throughout the world. It is an ideal pocket guide for the expert as well as being an excellent introduction for readers new to the subject. Equipment for basic and specialised purposes from Western Europe, Eastern Europe, the United States, Canada, Japan and elsewhere, is featured and the text is both readable and specifically technical and augmented by the many illustrations. Most of the world's major manufacturers are represented, as well as some unusual and less well-known ones.

About the Authors

Philip Porter lives in a Tudor farmhouse on the borders of Worcestershire, Herefordshire and Shropshire, where he has a fruit farm, writes books and edits a motoring magazine. His hobbies include ballooning, collecting old cars and membership of the Sherlock Holmes Society of London.

Nick Baldwin was brought up on a farm and his first job was working in the Land Rover factory. He has subsequently written several books and many articles on transport topics and he takes a special interest in farm tractors. He has a collection of old vehicles which includes a number of tractors.

As well as the paperback *New Observer's* guides, there are hardback *Observers* too, covering a wide range of topics.

NATURAL HISTORY Birds Birds' Eggs Wild Animals Farm Animals Sea Fishes Butterflies Larger Moths Caterpillars Sea and Seashore Cats Trees Grasses Cacti Gardens Roses House Plants Vegetables Geology Fossils

SPORT AND LEISURE Golf Tennis Sea Fishing Music Folk Song Jazz Big Bands Sewing Furniture Architecture Churches

COLLECTING Awards and Medals Glass Pottery and Porcelain Silver Victoriana Firearms Kitchen Antiques

TRANSPORT Small Craft Canals Vintage Cars Classic Cars Manned Spaceflight Unmanned Spaceflight

TRAVEL AND HISTORY London Devon and Cornwall Cotswolds World Atlas European Costume Ancient Britain Heraldry

The New Observer's Book of

Tractors and Farm Machinery

Compiled by
Philip Porter
and
Nick Baldwin

Frederick Warne

FREDERICK WARNE
Penguin Books Ltd, Harmondsworth, Middlesex, England
Viking Penguin Inc., 40 West 23rd Street, New York, New York 10010, U.S.A.
Penguin Books Australia Ltd, Ringwood, Victoria, Australia
Penguin Books Canada Ltd, 2801 John Street, Markham, Ontario, Canada L3R 1B4
Penguin Books (N.Z.) Ltd, 182–190 Wairau Road, Auckland 10, New Zealand

First published 1986

ISBN 0 7232 1689 4

Printed and bound in Great Britain by
Butler & Tanner Ltd
Frome and London

CONTENTS

AUTHORS' NOTE

In a book of this size it would be quite impossible to include every tractor and item of farm machinery manufactured in the world today. We have concentrated on trying to give a broad representation of the various types where information has been available to us.

The book begins with tractors, the most important single mechanical aid on the farm, and proceeds logically through machines for preparing the land, sowing the seed, harvesting the crop, and then concludes in a section on the increasingly popular farm materials handling machines and a wide variety of farm vehicles.

As farming methods and machinery become ever more sophisticated it becomes less obvious what machinery seen in the country may be engaged in, and so it is hoped that this book will help the general reader to keep abreast of such modern developments.

ACKNOWLEDGEMENTS

The authors would like to acknowledge the valuable assistance given by David Bradley, Andrew Yarnold, John Armstrong and David Rawkins; and by the various companies which provided information about their products.

TRACTORS

We look first at an assortment of tractors produced around the world. With some 100 makes to choose from we have selected types that represent the various sizes and categories of the available machines. We begin with compact machines that are widely used on small farms in southern Europe and the Far East, but are now finding specialist roles everywhere.

We move on to the classic shape that has evolved in the past 80 years. This is, of course, the type with large, driven rear wheels and small undriven front ones that steer. Next we examine the increasingly popular four-wheel drive types of similar configuration. These are able to transmit their power to the ground in heavy going with less slippage and therefore lower fuel consumption. Following these come four-wheel drive tractors with equal sized wheels at front and rear for maximum adhesion. As well as the compact types, these are available in the mid-horsepower range and are almost universal above the 200 hp level. As with the compact tractors, some steer at their front axles and some by pivoting in the middle. A few also steer at both front and rear for crab-tracking or, alternatively, to provide the smallest possible turning circle.

After the giants come the very efficient crawlers, whose use is limited only by their unsuitability for road use and their lower speeds. Before moving on to the implements that many of them work with we have a brief look at a few types of tractor designed for a special purpose, such as row crops, vineyards, mountain slopes, etc.

Virtually all the tractors have diesel engines and the vast majority have power take-offs capable of working towed or mounted machinery. Nearly all also have a hydraulic three-point linkage for handling implements and putting them to sophisticated use, as in the case of ploughs that require a delicate depth control.

Compact tractors

MAKE: FORD (UK)
MODEL: SERIES 10 Compact Tractors

Three-cylinder water-cooled diesel engines power the Series 10 compact tractors. The 1210 is rated at 16 hp, the 1710 provides 26 hp and the 1910 32 hp. The 1210 has 10 forward gears and 2 reverse, while the two larger models have 12 and 4. All have fully live hydraulics and Category I 3-point linkage. Four-wheel drive is also available.

MAKE: MITSUBISHI (Japan)
MODEL: MT 372 D

The compact tractors manufactured by Mitsubishi, the largest corporation in Japan, are aimed at commercial growers, local councils and industrial users apart from farmers. The MT 372 D is a 4-wheel drive, 15 hp water-cooled diesel tractor. It has a 3-step PTO system and a live hydraulic system enabling a wide range of implements to be fitted.

MAKE: KUBOTA (Japan)   MODEL: B7100DP

The Japanese firm of Kubota was formed in the 1890s and began manufacturing tractors in 1960. It claims to be the fifth largest producer in the world. The B7100DP is powered by a 3-cylinder diesel of 762 cc capacity which produces 16 hp. It is available with 4-wheel drive, independent rear brakes, and three-speed PTO.

MAKE: MASSEY FERGUSON (Multi-national)
MODEL: MF 1010

The MF 1010 with the MF 1020 and MF 1030 form a range of compact tractors that are small and manoeuvrable yet rugged and versatile. They are made with either 2- or 4-wheel drive and are used on smallholdings, parks, larger gardens or golf courses. They are particularly good for yard scraping, soil preparation outside and inside glasshouses and tunnels, all systems of grass mowing and turf maintenance, plus materials handling. They are fitted with a 3-cylinder diesel engine of either 16, 21 or 27 hp, dependent on model.

MAKE: ISEKI (Japan)   MODEL: TX 2140/2160

The Iseki 2140 and 2160 models are small compact tractors but they have many of the features found on the larger more sophisticated models. They are primarily used for farms, estates, smallholdings, parks and sports grounds. Offered in 2- and 4-wheel drive versions, they are powered by a 3-cylinder water-cooled engine. Balanced weight distribution minimizes floating and sinking of the front wheels and prevents spinning and slipping. Acceleration can be controlled through both a hand lever and a foot pedal. The TX 2140, with a 776 cc engine, and the TX 2160, with an 849 cc unit, can be fitted with a wide range of British made attachments including a backhoe, loader, and rotary, gang and flail mowers.

MAKE: HINOMOTO (Japan)   MODEL: C174

The Hinomoto C174 is a small 4-wheel drive tractor from Japan. It has a 3-cylinder indirect-injection, water-cooled diesel engine of 1004 cc capacity. It produces 20 hp and has glow plugs for cold starting. It weighs just 658 kg, and has a rear mounted PTO and hydraulic linkage. It has 9 forward and 3 reverse gears.

13

MAKE: HOLDER (West Germany)
MODEL: Cultitrac A40

The Holder A40 was designed for working in narrow row spacings and tight conditions. It has hydraulically operated articulated steering and 4-wheel drive, giving it good manoeuvrability and traction even over uneven ground. With a width of just one metre and a wide range of implements, it is a very versatile small tractor.

MAKE: HOWARD (Australia)   MODEL: 200

Made in Australia by the inventor of the Rotavator rotary cultivator, this diminutive 10 hp tractor uses a 375 cc Briggs and Stratton petrol, TVO or LPG engine. It has PTO and implement lift and is intended specifically for farm work rather than simply as a lawn tractor. Howard have a British company but this manufactures implements rather than tractors.

MAKE: GRILLO (Italy)   MODEL: 31

There are at least 12 Italian makers of small 4 × 4 tractors. Some have centre-pivot steering whilst others, like this Grillo, have king pins on their front axles for steering. Grillo manufacture pivot steer types as well. The 31 is available with 26–40 hp, 2- or 3-cylinder air-cooled diesels and 5 or 6 forward ratio gearboxes.

Diesel crawler tractor

V 228
230
232

**MAKE: BLANK (West Germany)
MODEL: V228**

Made in Germany but also typical of the very small crawlers made particularly in Italy, this Blank is used for vineyard cultivation. It has a 2-cylinder air-cooled 25 hp diesel engine with 6 forward gears. There is an implement lift and 540 rpm PTO. Steering is by lever-controlled clutches and brakes.

General tractors

MAKE: MARSHALL (UK)   MODEL: 502

The 502 is a general purpose farm workhorse and is also popular with local authorities for municipal work. It is powered by a 3-cylinder 47 hp diesel and has a number of features normally found only on the more powerful tractors. It has a synchro gearbox giving 3 forward gears and 1 reverse in high, medium and low ranges.

MAKE: MARSHALL (UK)   MODEL: 800 Series

Powered by a turbocharged 4-cylinder diesel producing 82 hp, the 800 Series is Marshall's top of the range tractor. It has a self adjusting heavy duty 305 mm clutch, fully live hydraulic system, multi-speed PTO drive, oil immersed brakes and the advanced Explorer cab. It is also available with 4-wheel drive and creep gears giving speeds down to 0.3 mph.

MAKE: LAMBORGHINI (Italy)   MODEL: 956

The Italian Lamborghini 956 has a water-cooled modular type engine of 5499 cc which gives 95 hp. The front axle has disc brakes and a steering angle of up to 50 degrees. The hydraulic power lift has a capacity 4600 kg and a draught and position control. The 956 DT is a 4wd version.

MAKE: VOLVO BM VALMET (Sweden)
MODEL: 805

The 805 is one of the larger tractors manufactured by Volvo in Sweden. It has a turbocharged 4-cylinder unit which gives 95 hp and is designed for the heavier jobs in agriculture and forestry. The power train and fuel tank are enclosed within the large, sturdy box section chassis. The 4wd version is named the 805-4.

MAKE: CASE (Multi-national)   MODEL: 685L

The Case company took over David Brown Tractors in 1972 and now manufacture these medium sized tractors in Britain for export to the States. More recently Case amalgamated with International Harvester. The 685L is a 69 hp 4-cylinder tractor with synchromesh 8 forward and 4 reverse transmission with hydrostatic power steering and independent dual speed PTO.

MAKE: CASE (Multi-national)   MODEL: 1594

The 1594 is offered with the option of Hydra-Shift semi-automatic transmission which gives the choice of

4 gears in each of 4 ranges—creep, field, road or reverse—whilst moving. It is driven by a 96 hp 6-cylinder engine and has advanced hydraulics with lower link sensing which handles variations in draught loading.

MAKE: SAME (Italy)   MODEL: Condor 55

The SAME concern, which was started in Italy in 1942, now owns Lamborghini. The 2827 cc capacity SAME 1003 P engine is a direct injection air cooled diesel of 3-cylinders and produces 55 hp. It has a lower link depth sensing control and an interlock device preventing the engine from starting when gears are engaged.

MAKE: SAME (Italy)   MODEL: 90 & 100

The 90 and 100 models have many features in common. Both have mechanical transmission with 12 forward and 3 reverse gears, and a maximum speed of 18.6 mph. Both have reactive-type hydrostatic steering, a 70 degree steering angle, a load sensing control and a 540 rpm and 1000 rpm PTO. The 90 produces 88 hp and the 100, 100 hp.

MAKE: UNIVERSAL (Rumania)   MODEL: 1010

Universal tractors are made in Brasov, Rumania, and began production in 1946. Three-quarters of its production is exported to over 80 countries and in North America they are known under the name Long. The 1010 is fitted with a 5393 cc 4-stroke, direct injection 6-cylinder diesel which produces 100 hp.

MAKE: CHAMBERLAIN (Australia)
MODEL: 4480B Sedan

Chamberlain is an Australian tractor manufacturer which is now 49 per cent owned by John Deere. It began production in 1947 and still makes its own tractors as well as selling John Deere's. As is usual Australian practice, the 4480B has no hydraulics but an adjustable swinging drawbar. It has a John Deere 5.88 litre turbocharged diesel.

MAKE: MASSEY FERGUSON (Multi-national)
MODEL: MF 200 Series

The MF 200 Series is a range of medium horsepower tractors which are competitively priced. Available as the MF 230, MF 240, MF 250, MF 265 and MF 290 they produce 38 hp, 45 hp, 47 hp, 60 hp and 77 hp respectively. The first two are 2-wheel drive only, whilst the last three have the option of 4-wheel drive if required. All have Perkins engines and Ferguson system hydraulics for simple precise control. The 4-wheel drive versions of the MF 260 and MF 290 are fitted with, in addition to the rear axle differential lock, a front axle self-actuating differential lock which is claimed virtually to eliminate front wheelspin.

MAKE: MASSEY FERGUSON (Multi-national)
MODEL: MF 600 Series

The MF 600 Series consists of four models ranging in output from 69 to 100 hp. Each has the option of 2- or 4-wheel drive, Perkins engines, synchromesh transmission and high performance PTO (power take off) systems. Particular attention has been paid to cab design to ensure good protection and comfort for the driver. The MF 675 is the bottom of the range model with a 3900 cc engine. The next model up is the most popular, the MF 690, with a 4060 cc 4-cylinder engine producing 83 hp and good low speed torque. The MF 698T is powered by a turbocharged version of the 3.9 engine and produces 94 hp. Top of the range is the MF 699 with a smooth 6-cylinder engine of 5800 cc.

MAKE: DEUTZ-FAHR (West Germany)
MODEL: DX3

The DX 3.70 and DX 3.90 have engines of 3770 cc and 4085 cc respectively. Both have the option of 4-wheel drive, and helical gearing in the transmission ensures easy changing of the fully synchromesh 12 forward and 4 reverse gears. The Deutz diesel engine is air cooled and designed for many years of tough service. The smaller engine produces 76 hp and the larger, 82 hp. Particular attention has been paid to comfort and the Starcab has a clear, logical layout of instruments and controls together with large panoramic windows. Powerful hydraulics, called the Transfermatic System, and efficient PTO shafts, plus an optional front PTO shaft, complete the specification.

MAKE: RENAULT (France)   MODEL: 61 RS

Designed for operation in confined areas, the 61 RS has a low profile with the over-all height of the cab being just 2.5 metres, allowing it to be used in and around low buildings. A 3-cylinder diesel engine develops 60 hp and gives a maximum 57 hp at the PTO. The cab tilts for maintenance.

MAKE: RENAULT (France)   MODEL: 80 TX

This 78 hp tractor is powered by a 4-cylinder water cooled diesel giving 78 hp. It is available in both 2- and 4-wheel drive versions with a transmission giving 12 forward and 12 reverse gears, plus a synchronized forward-reverse lever for shuttle operations. Hydrostatic steering is standard as are the twin disc brakes.

MAKE: MARSHALL (UK)   MODEL: 904XL

The 904XL is a 4-wheel drive tractor for heavier farm jobs. Power is provided by a 4-cylinder turbocharged 92 hp diesel with a torque ratio of 240 lbs/ft at 1600 engine rpm. The 2-speed PTO gives 83 hp at 2200 rpm and the dual assistor rams give a maximum hydraulic lift of 2880 kg. The luxury cab ensures good visibility.

MAKE: FORD (UK)   MODEL: 4610

Basildon, in Essex, UK, is the centre of Ford world-wide tractor production. It is the largest of 8 manufacturing and assembly plants located around the world and exports to 75 countries. The 10 Series consists of 11 tractors ranging from the 2900 cc 44 hp 2910 model to the 6600 cc 115 hp 8210. The 4610 is powered by a 3300 cc 64 hp unit.

MAKE: FORD (UK)   MODEL: 7610

The 7610 is a member of the 10 Series range which produces 12 per cent more power than the previous range, yet uses 6 per cent less fuel. The front wheels can turn 50 degrees and the limited slip differential engages automatically under slippery conditions. The 4400 cc engine gives 103 hp, and the 7610 is fitted with double acting draught control and load monitor.

MAKE: FORD (UK)   MODEL: TW Series

The TW Series consists of the TW15, TW25 and TW35. All are fitted with a turbocharged 6-cylinder diesel engine of 6610 cc displacement. The power produced ranges from 143 hp for the TW15 to 195 hp for the TW35. A variable speed viscous fan conserves engine power and fuel. Four-wheel drive with centre mounted differential is optional on the TW15 and TW25, and standard on the TW35. It can be engaged on the move from a switch in the cab, which has been designed for maximum comfort. The heavy duty hydraulic linkage provides 4556 kg lift capacity and separate pumps supply the driveline components and the power steering.

MAKE: VOLVO BM VALMET (Sweden)
MODEL: 2105

In 1972 Volvo of Sweden and Valmet of Finland merged their tractor interests to develop the Nordic range for the Scandinavian countries. The 2105 is the largest in the range and is powered by a 6-cylinder turbocharged diesel with intercooling with an output of 163 hp. Attention has been given to excluding noise, vibration and dust from the cab.

MAKE: MARSHALL (UK)   MODEL: 100 Series

The Marshall 100 features a high-tech hydraulic system fully electronically controlled from a cab mounted console. This provides the facility to mix draught and position control plus a variable response to lift and lower. Lift capacity is 4536 kg and it is powered by the 103 hp Leyland 6/98 6-cylinder engine. The luxury cab is ergonomically designed for comfort and efficiency.

MAKE: ZETOR (Czechoslovakia)
MODEL: 8045 Crystal

Zetor is a Czechoslovakian company. Versions are assembled in various countries including Iraq, India, Burma, Argentina, Uruguay and the Congo. The 8045 is a 4-wheel drive tractor with a four-cylinder 4562 cc diesel engine which develops 85 hp and drives through 8 forward and 4 reverse gears plus a torque multiplier.

MAKE: MASSEY FERGUSON (Multi-national)
MODEL: 2005 Series

The MF 2005 Series consists of 3 large tractors all powered by a 5800 cc Perkins diesel engine which develops maximum torque at very low revs. Together with good power output this ensures excellent traction and economy, the minimum of gear changing and wheelspin. The MF 2645 produces 117 hp and the MF 2685 is turbocharged with an output of 142 hp. Top model of this trio is the MF 2725, which is both turbocharged and charge-cooled, producing 158 hp as a result. All models have 4-wheel drive, push button electro hydraulic actuation of front and rear differential locks and no less than 16 forward and 12 reverse gears.

MAKE: DEUTZ-FAHR (West Germany)
MODEL: DX 4

The DX 4 series consists of the DX 4.30, DX 4.50 and the DX 4.70. All three are powered by 4-cylinder 4085 cc air-cooled diesel engines produced by Deutz, who claim to be the largest manufacturer of diesel engines in the world. The DX 4.30 has an output of 82 hp and, like the other models, drum brakes, fully synchronized transmission and the Transfermatic system of hydraulics. The DX 4.50 and DX 4.70 are both turbocharged and are available with 4-wheel drive. All models have 15 forward and 5 reverse gears. For operator comfort the engine is sound proofed and the cab mounted on rubber.

MAKE: DEUTZ-FAHR (West Germany)
MODEL: DX 7.10

The DX 7.10 is the largest tractor made by the German company Deutz-Fahr. All 4 wheels are driven by a 6-cylinder 6128 cc air-cooled diesel which in turbocharged form has a power output of 170 hp. The front axle is fitted with an Optitrac self-locking differential and Powermatic transmission.

MAKE: BELARUS (USSR)   MODEL: 862 D

The Russian Belarus 862 tractor is designed for high speed field work. It is suitable for conditions where power can be used effectively and time is important. With a 90 hp engine it can be used for both cultivation and haulage. The 862 has an automatic 4-wheel drive system that operates only when it is needed. When the rear wheels slip approximately 6 per cent, the front-wheel drive engages. The 4075 cc 4-cylinder engine operates through 18 forward and 2 reverse gears, all of which are controlled by one lever. Other features include Hydrostatic steering, twin external assistor rams, and a synchronized braking system. The 862 D is fitted with independent and ground speed PTO and has full Category II live hydraulics with draught and position control.

MAKE: JOHN DEERE (USA)
MODEL: 1640/2040/2140

The 1640/2040/2140 series of tractors by John Deere are all powered by a 4-cylinder 3.9 litre diesel engine. The 1640 develops 62 hp, the 2040 70 hp, and the 2140 74 hp. These engines feature replaceable wet-type cylinder liners, under piston spray cooling and a strong crankshaft with 5 main bearings. These tractors are fitted with a hand adjusted Load and Depth Control device which automatically senses the weight and length of attached implements and adapts for varying soil conditions to improve tillage results. The low profile cab allows the tractor to pass through low doors and has sound absorbent, non-glare insulation.

MAKE: RENAULT (France)   MODEL: 106-14

The Renault 106-14 has a 6-cylinder engine developing 96 hp from its 5656 cc unit. It is available in 4-wheel drive and has 12 forward and 12 reverse gears. The tilting cab has good visibility, wide-opening lockable doors and easy to operate controls. It is claimed to have ample power for the majority of field operations.

MAKE: FIAT (Italy)   MODEL: 45-66

The Fiat 45-66 is powered by a 3-cylinder 2710 cc engine which produces 45 hp. The 'Q' cab is independently mounted on rubber blocks thereby improving comfort and reducing noise and vibration. It has a rear PTO and hydraulic lift. The DT model has a special front axle designed to achieve a steering angle of 45 degrees.

MAKE: FIAT (Italy)   MODEL: 80-90

The Medium 90 series consists of 4 models: the 55-90, the 60-90, the 70-90, and the 80-90. In each case the first two numbers refer to the horsepower rating. The engine sizes, respectively, are 2710 cc, 2931 cc, 3613 cc and 3908 cc, the first two being 3-cylinder units, the latter two being 4-cylinder. Good front wheel grip is assisted by the favourable weight distribution and long wheelbase. The centrally mounted transmission shaft, coaxial with the gearbox, has no universal joints. Fiat claim to produce the biggest selling tractor in Europe and the largest range of 2- and 4-wheel drive tractors available today. Together with Laverda combine harvesters and Hesston mowers and balers, they make up the Fiatagri group. Fiat Trattori first started producing and marketing tractors in 1919.

MAKE: FIAT (Italy)   MODEL: 130-90

Like the Medium 90 series, the Big 90 series consists of several models with increasing outputs. These are the 115-90, 130-90, 140-90, 160-90 and 180-90. All but the 115-90 are turbocharged. The 130-90 has a 6-cylinder 5861 cc engine and is water cooled. Using the creeper speed Super-reduction unit, the 130-90 will crawl along at just 0.12 mph.

MAKE: JOHN DEERE (USA)   MODEL: 4450

A large 7.6 litre 6-cylinder diesel engine, developing 160 hp, powers the John Deere 4450. It is a turbo-charged unit and features mechanical front-wheel drive when required. The transmission has a 15-speed power shift allowing the operator to use a single lever to start up, slow down, and reverse direction without using the clutch.

MAKE: COUNTY (UK)   MODEL: 774 & 974

County Tractors manufacture a range of equal wheel

4-wheel drive tractors based on Ford power trains. Used throughout the world in agriculture, forestry and civil engineering, County Tractors have twin drive shafts powering the front hubs from the rear axles. The 774 is based on the 86 hp Ford 6610, and the 974 on the 103 hp turbocharged Ford 7610. The County system of transmission to four equally sized large wheels gives, it is claimed, a number of advantages. These include, lower more evenly balanced ground pressures, lower centre of gravity for excellent stability, good ground clearance, improved safety as brakes are effective on all 4 wheels and the higher tractive effort associated with equal 4-wheel drive. County Tractors also have a single differential with lock operating on all 4 wheels.

MAKE: COUNTY (UK)   MODEL: 764

The County 764 is powered by a 4386 cc 4-cylinder direct injection overhead valve diesel manufactured by Ford. It produces 86 hp, and with its dual range transmission has 8 forward and 2 reverse gears. The wheels may be set to suit any track from 1.6 m to 2.1 m in steps of 102 mm.

MAKE: COUNTY (UK)   MODEL: 1474 & 1884

The 1474 has the 163 hp 6-cylinder turbocharged Ford TW 25 power unit and the 1884 has the turbocharged and intercooled TW 35 which produces 195 hp, making it the most powerful in the County range. Both have Cat II hydraulic lift linkage with bottom link sensing and a constant mesh dual range, dual power gearbox with 16 forward and 4 reverse gears.

MAKE: HOLDER (West Germany)
MODEL: A60

The Holder 4-wheel drive skidder Cultitrac A60 is an ideal machine for thinning forestry. Being articulated makes it extremely manoeuvrable, and combined with the all-wheel drive and equally sized wheels gives excellent traction in the most difficult conditions. The articulated steering gives good stability and therefore safety from overturning. The tractor is compact in size and has a good power-to-weight ratio being powered by a specially developed 3-cylinder water cooled engine. To avoid compacting the soil whilst cultivating or spraying, the A60 has a slight weight bias to the front so that using a rear mounted attachment does not upset the weight balance between front and rear. It has frameless unit construction and the all-synchromesh transmission gives speeds from $\frac{1}{2}$ to 15 mph. A turbocharged version is also available.

MAKE: MERCEDES BENZ (West Germany)
MODEL: MB-trac 800

The Mercedes Benz MB-trac 800 is the most popular 4-wheel drive tractor in the MB-trac range. It has a chassis frame and 4 equal sized wheels for maximum traction. Most of the weight is concentrated over the front axle to offset the effect of rear mounted implements. It is powered by a 3780 cc 4-stroke diesel and produces 75 hp.

MAKE: MERCEDES BENZ (West Germany)
MODEL: MB-trac 1500

An interesting feature of the heavy duty range, including the MB-trac 1500, is that, being fully reversible, they can be dual directional. A compact console consisting of the steering wheel, all instruments and controls, foot pedals and the seat can, as an optional extra, revolve through 180 degrees so that the tractor may be easily driven in either direction. All forward gears are reversible and the tractor can replace specialist self-propelled machinery. The MB-trac 1500 pulls, pushes, carries and propels implements, being fitted with a turbocharged version of the 5675 cc engine which develops 150 hp.

Giant

MAKE: FORD (USA)   MODEL: FW-60

The largest Ford tractor is the massive FW-60. It is powered by a 325 hp Cummins turbocharged, after-cooled engine of 14,061 cc. Peak torque is 1080 lb/ft at 1400 rpm and a constant mesh or automatic gearbox is offered. Articulated hydrostatic steering, a lift capacity of 5670 kg and air conditioning are all standard. The height is 3.42 m and the width is 4.17 m.

MAKE: KIROV (USSR)   MODEL: K-701

This 12-ton giant is manufactured in Russia. It has

a 4-stroke liquid cooled V12 diesel which delivers 300 hp. This engine features a liquid vibration damper on the front end of the crankshaft and roller main bearings. The engine oil pump is driven by an electric motor which is switched on immediately before starting to build up required pressure in the lubricating system. Torque is transmitted to the gearbox by a semi-rigid coupling with a reduction unit. The coupling can be disengaged for starting the engine in cold weather. The mechanically controlled planetary gearbox has hydraulically controlled friction clutches giving speed changing without breaking the flow of power. For fuel economy the rear axle can also be disengaged when not required. The articulated frame turns in two planes to aid traction.

MAKE: MASSEY FERGUSON (Multi-national)
MODEL: MF 4880

The MF 4880 is fitted with a Cummins VT903 engine which produces 307 hp from its 14,800 cc displacement. Steering is Hydrostatic power assisted and of the pivot type which articulates 42 degrees in either direction and oscillates 30 degrees in total. Capacities in litres are: coolant 56.8, engine crankcase 35.5, rear axle 79.5 and steering reservoir 90.8.

MAKE: CAMECO (USA)   MODEL: 405 B

Cameco is a US company from Louisiana, the sugar
cane territory. The 405 B uses a Caterpillar 3306 D.I.T.
engine of 10,500 cc which gives 250 hp and drives
through an Allison constant mesh spur type planetary
automatic transmission. The frame, which articulates
45 degrees and oscillates 22 degrees, is made of 19 mm
thick steel plate. The 505 B has a 325 hp turbocharged
14,700 cc engine.

MAKE: JOHN DEERE (USA)
MODEL: 8450/8650/8850

The 8450, 8650 and 8850 tractors are the largest

made by John Deere and have 4-wheel drive. The 8450 has a 6-cylinder 7.6 litre engine turbocharged and intercooled producing 225 hp. The 8650 has a larger 10.1 litre unit which develops 290 hp and the 8850 a massive V8 15.6 litre unit with 4 valves per cylinder which produces no less than 370 hp. Both are fitted with turbochargers and intercoolers. These tractors are articulated, which means they steer by bending at a centre hinge. An advantage of this, apart from improved turning, is that the rear wheels always follow the tracks of the front ones.

MAKE: KNUDSON (USA)   MODEL: 4360

The massive Knudson, developed in the United States in the 1970s for hillside work, is powered by a 14,000 cc Cummins 6-cylinder which produces 360 hp. It has independent or integrated steering on each axle and microprocessors to keep the engine and cab level on slopes of up to 28 degrees, plus microprocessor-controlled Twin Disc transmission.

MAKE: ALLIS-CHALMERS (USA)
MODEL: 4W-305

The American Allis-Chalmers company began tractor manufacture in 1913 and in the 1930s were pioneers of pneumatic tyres and, in the 1940s, torque-convertor transmission. Today they have an alliance with the Fiat concern. The 4W-305 has a twin turbocharged, 4 valves per cylinder 305 hp engine with 20 forward and 4 reverse gears and a column-mounted range shift.

MAKE: STEIGER (USA)
MODEL: TIGER ST-470

The US Steiger is part owned by International

Harvester, now merged with Case, and manufactures tractors under licence for Ford. It specializes in large tractors and the largest in the range is the Tiger ST-470. It has a 470 hp Cummins power plant and produces 387 hp at the drawbar. It weighs no less than 18,462 kg.

Crawlers

MAKE: TRACK MARSHALL (UK)
MODEL: TM135

The TM135 can handle large implements even in poor conditions. It develops 136 hp through its 6-cylinder Perkins diesel and it has a drawbar pull of 10,144 kg at 2.04 mph in first gear. The ground pressure, however, complete with cab, 3-point linkage and counterweights is less than 10 lbs/sq. in. The TM135 is the most popular crawler tractor in the UK.

MAKE: TRACK MARSHALL (UK)
MODEL: Britannia

The Britannia is a compact crawler designed to be an economical answer to all weather cultivation. The 70.6 hp Perkins and carefully chosen gear ratios enable it to exert a drawbar pull of 9389 kg whilst avoiding compaction or ground smear problems. The single lever steering is hydraulically operated and allows gradual, controlled turning or sharp turns as required.

MAKE: CATERPILLAR (USA)
MODEL: Crawler Range

Caterpillar manufacture 3 specifically agricultural

tractors entitled the D4E VHP, D5B VHP and D6D VHP. They all feature the famous crawler tracks first developed by the firm's forerunners in 1904. The VHP stands for variable horsepower, a new development in tillage tractors. The engine operates at its standard rating in first and second gears, but fuel supply is increased in third gear and above to give a greater power output. On the D6D this increases drawbar pull by 27–37 per cent above 3 mph and gives a productivity increase of up to 40 per cent. The power ranges are, D4E, 97–125 hp from 7 litre turbocharged engine, D5B, 60–120 hp from 10.5 litres turbocharged and D6D, 165–216 hp from the same unit with an aftercooler.

MAKE: MASSEY FERGUSON (Multi-national)
MODEL: MF 234C

Where traction, stability and restricted space are problems, the Massey Ferguson MF 234C crawler tractor can provide the solution. It is well suited to nursery and orchard work and especially where sticky ground could well cause damage and costly delays with conventionally rubber tyred tractors. Despite this model's narrow width, good traction and stability are maintained because of the double tracks.

MAKE: FIATAGRI (Italy)   MODEL: 70-65

Fiatagri claim to be the largest manufacturer of agricultural crawler tractors in the world. In the 70–65, power output at the flywheel of 70 hp is produced by the 4-cylinder 3613 cc diesel. The 2 steering clutches are operated by hand levers and the band type brakes work on the steering clutch drums.

MAKE: TRACTOROEXPORT (USSR)
MODEL: T-70C

The T-70C is manufactured in Russia and is of the

caterpillar type. It is designed to mechanize the whole operation of cultivating and harvesting sugar beet and other cultivated crops. It can be used for ploughing, harrowing, stubble ploughing, sowing, fertilizing and harvesting, and is driven by a 70 hp motor.

Specialized

MAKE: RENAULT (France)   MODEL: S Series

The Renault S Series are known as Orchard Tractors and used extensively in the vineyards of France. No less than 7 different models are available powered by 3- and 4-cylinder in-line engines ranging from the 2552 cc 48 hp Renault 70S to the 3770 cc 65 hp Renault 656S. The linkage fitted is a 3-point vineyard type.

MAKE: JOHN DEERE (USA)
MODEL: 1140 Narrow Tractor

The 1140 Narrow Tractor is specially adapted for orchard and vineyard work. Though a compact tractor it has many of the features of a larger tractor. It has a high torque large displacement engine that delivers 56 hp and a 3-point hydraulic hitch. Various transmissions are offered to suit the operators' requirements.

MAKE: COUNTY (UK)
MODEL: 1184 Forward Control

The 1184 Forward Control tractor can be used with

a wide range of carried equipment as well as linkage mounted and trailer implements. It is powered by a 120 hp Ford engine. The forward mounted cab imposes sufficient weight on the front axle to balance the unit for maximum traction during heavy draught operations.

MAKE: ISEKI (Japan)   MODEL: T6500 H/C

Modern farmers may need to apply solid or liquid chemicals late in the growing season. With this in mind, Iseki have developed a special high clearance tractor. It is fitted with equal size wheel equipment all round, powered front axle, and has a ground clearance in excess of 694 mm. It is powered by a water-cooled, 4-cylinder diesel of 3595 cc displacement. The transmission is of the constant mesh type, fully synchromesh, with 20 forward and 5 reverse gears. Skid units are also available if required. The Japanese Iseki company also manufactures tractors for Bolens and WFE.

MAKE: COUNTY (UK)   MODEL: 762H

The high drive 762H is particularly suitable for row crop work including the mounting of spray equipment. The high clearance transmission is by a vertical train of gears housed in a heavy casing allowing full engine power to be used. This tractor, based on the Ford 6600, has under axle height of 0.9 m with row crop tyres.

MAKE: VALMET (Finland)
MODEL: Jehu 1122

Valmet, the Finnish company now amalgamated with Volvo of Sweden, manufactures a special tractor for use in forestry. The Jehu 1122 has 'tracks' for improved traction in deep snow and a cab-mounted hydraulic jib and grabber for handling felled tree trunks, which are then carried in its trailer.

MAKE: CAMOXOAHOE (USSR)
MODEL: T-16M

The Russian T-16M is a tool-frame tractor to which implements such as hoes can be mid-mounted. The very short cab is positioned over the rear wheels and a platform body with sides can be mounted on the front for carrying silage, etc. Its high frame gives it good ground clearance for use in row crops.

MAKE: BUCHER (Switzerland)
MODEL: Tractomobil TM1000

Thanks to the excellent characteristics of the Tractomobil on slopes and its power steering, reliable brakes and the short, compact construction, it permits safe operation on very steep and rough ground. The Tractomobil, powered by a Leyland 48 hp diesel, is a versatile vehicle not only for forage harvesting on mountains, foothill and lowland farms, but also for arable farming, crop tending and for towing and transport work. The powerful front-mounted hydraulic system with standardized 3-point fixing permits the use of many front-mounted attachments. The capability of hydraulically moving the front-mounted lifting unit sideways affords special advantages. It allows trees and other obstacles to be smoothly avoided when the implement projects beyond the width of the tractor. It has selectable 4-wheel drive, differential locks and 16 gears.

MAKE: BOBARD (France) MODEL: B45 Poly Bob

Bobard, a French company, specialize in manufacturing tractors for cultivating tall crops and vines. They sell 700 tractors a year including the curious Poly Bob.

This has two equally-sized driven and steered wheels placed in line, and steadying wheels on either side adjustable for row width. The Alsace machine can clear crops 3 m high.

MAKE: CBT (Brazil)   MODEL: 3000

CBT is a Brazilian company and the version seen here is being used for cane handling. It is powered by a Dodge V8 made under licence by Volkswagen in Brazil and these engines are run on locally produced vegetable alcohol. With a capacity of 5212 cc, the engine develops 108 hp. Unusually, today, CBTs are frame built.

MAKE: BUCHER (Switzerland)
MODEL: Tractomobil TM 800

The Swiss-made Bucher is designed for use on steep sloping fields and uneven terrain. Four-wheel steering and permanently engaged all-wheel drive mean less damage to ground surface and a tight turning circle. The low centre of gravity wide-track design and low pressure tyres provide stability. A 24 hp Kubota 3-cylinder provides the motive force.

MAKE: RASANT (West Germany)
MODEL: Berg-Trak

Rasant is a West German company which specializes in manufacturing special low-profile tractors for use by farmers in mountainous regions. They are available with 4 or 6 driven wheels and use MAG engines. The Berg-Trak has a 750 cc 2-cylinder 18 hp engine and has two independent PTOs. It can work on slopes as steep as 60 degrees.

MAKE: COUNTY (UK)   MODEL: 754

This Ford 75 hp engined model with its rear cab is also built as a special tractor for working on boggy ground. For maximum flotation the equal sized driving wheels are covered with detachable open mesh FIN tracks whose ground pressure is further reduced by being stretched over small front idler wheels. The example shown is cutting drainage ditches on a peat moor.

MAKE: BLANK (West Germany)
MODEL: Stilt-Tractors

Several firms in America and Europe make ultra high clearance tractors for working in tall row crops. The 35 hp example made by Karl Blank KG is intended specially for rose cultivation. It can straddle 2 rows and has a powered tool bar in the centre which enables it to trim, hoe and even pick the blooms when special equipment is added.

PREPARING THE LAND

The varied machinery used to prepare the land for growing crops is mainly towed by or attached to tractors. This preparation for the agricultural cycle may be carried out occasionally, or annually, and sometimes more often in the course of a year.

The dispersal of excess water can be a problem in wet climates and in certain soil conditions. Excessively wet soil makes it difficult for tractors and machinery to work without getting bogged down and compressing the soil. Too much water in the soil retards plant growth because the air space that roots need in the soil is occupied by the water. The simplest method of draining the ground is to use a mole plough, which cuts a narrow but deep channel to guide the water to ditches or to the main drainage system of perforated pipes, which are laid by a more sophisticated machine.

Historically, hedging was a cheaper alternative to fencing and today there are a variety of machines made for cutting hedges speedily.

Land can be improved by the application of manure, slurry and chemical fertilizers. There are a variety of machines to spread these, from the traditional muck-spreader to the broadcaster which distributes via a spinning device, and to the injector which forces the fertilizer into the ground.

To break up the top layer of soil to give the roots of plants a chance to penetrate the soil, the farmer uses a plough. In principle these have changed little over the centuries and still cut and invert the top layer. Today the plough, instead of being drawn, is attached to the tractor's 3-point linkage and the depth and attitude are carefully and sometimes automatically controlled. The development of the reversible plough allows the ploughman to work adjacent rows by revolving the plough and turning the soil the same way in spite of travelling in the opposite direction.

The farmer will want to reduce a rough-ploughed field to a suitable seedbed. To achieve this there are a wide variety of cultivators and harrows to break down the earth. Stone-clearers remove the large stones that inhibit growth and threaten to damage machinery. Rollers are used to break down clods and for firming the seedbed when required.

Drainage machines

MAKE: MICHAEL MOORE (UK)   MODEL: Easy Mole

Unchanged for over 100 years, the mole plough drainage concept has been developed by Michael Moore, one of the world's leading mole plough designers and manufacturers. Incorporating double beams, giving greater stability and cutting down draught, allows the use of a wide range of towing tractors of 80 hp and upwards. The use of wheels reduces the cutting draught further.

MAKE: WESTMAC (UK)
MODEL: Rotary Ditcher D 2000

The D 2000 is designed for cleaning and making ditches at speed. The 6 rotor blades cope with many of the obstructions found in ditches, e.g. stones, roots, weeds and trash, allowing ditches up to 1 metre in depth to be tackled. New ditches can be cut in one or more passes with this tractor mounted machine.

MAKE: DAISY D (UK)   MODEL: Drainer

The Daisy D drainer is claimed to be a fast and simple method of laying flexible pipes under normal soil conditions. It fits the hydraulics of any standard tractor and opens the trench, lays the pipe, surrounds it with gravel, and closes the trench again. It is claimed to give a cost saving of 74 per cent over conventional equipment.

MAKE: BRUFF (UK)   MODEL: TG7 Trenchless

The self-propelled trenchless drainer, powered by a 280 hp engine and built on a special pivoting frame, is a robust, powerful machine designed to work in arduous conditions and to achieve high outputs. This method of laying drainage pipe (exclusively plastic) is very efficient, with outputs up to 6 km/day in good soil conditions. Trenchless is normally used with gravel (porous fill), so the machine requires a cart to deliver the gravel and to work in unison. There has been a trend to reduce the distance between laterals to 10 m or even 8 m, instead of the normal 20 m spacing, and leave out the gravel. This is difficult if there is an old scheme of clay pipes in the ground, as it is necessary to connect these into the new scheme. Where gravel is used this is automatically achieved. The gravel cost is up to 60 per cent of the whole job.

MAKE: BRUFF (UK)   MODEL: BT4 Trencher

The BT4 is a trencher of 168 hp which cuts a narrow 114 mm trench into which can be laid 60 or 80 mm diameter laterals with or without gravel. The trench is cut with a heavy duty chain onto which are bolted cutters. The movement of the cutters on the soil and the wear on the chain drive sprockets is expensive in spares, therefore the trenchless system is initially more expensive but cheaper to run. Farmers, however, may need convincing of the benefits of the trenchless as they like to see into an open trench and see the old systems connected up. To fill the open trench, the Trencher is fitted with an angled blade known as a *back fill blade*. Plastic pipe now accounts for at least 70 per cent, with the remainder being clay.

Hedge trimmers

MAKE: McCONNEL (UK)   MODEL: PA35

The McConnel PA35 is both a flail hedger and a verge mower. It can be used on any tractor from 45 hp upwards and is easily interchangeable for left or right-hand cutting. The PA35 has its own independent hydraulics, having 2 pumps mounted in tandem on the tractor's PTO shaft. A compact electric control panel can be mounted anywhere in the cab, and 3 switches give the operator instant and precise movement of reach, height and angle. The geometry features a parallel arm which can automatically adjust the angle irrespective of the adjustment to the reach. If the 1·2 m wide flail meets an obstruction it automatically swings up and back, returning to the working position once the obstruction is passed. The arm can be moved within the tractor's width for transporting.

MAKE: LELY (UK)   MODEL: Hedgehoppers

The Hedgehopper is a versatile machine which can be used for flail cutting of hedges, verges and ditch clearing. It can also, with appropriate attachments, be used for sawing or slashing enabling the Hedgehopper to cut through heavy growth and trees up to 305 mm diameter. The Tufcut model has a reach of 3.8 m and the Procut, 5 m.

MAKE: TURNER (UK)
MODEL: Hydramower 15, 18 & 23

The Hydramowers are available in a variety of sizes with the model number denoting the length of reach in feet. There is a choice of mid-mounting or rear-mounting, with the latter being able to be fitted or removed from the tractor in just 10 minutes. The standard cutting head with its upward cutting action is well suited to grass and light shrub. There is also a circular saw attachment for use in forestry and land reclamation. A 52 hp hydraulic system, protected by a release valve, is fitted as standard. A quickly detachable 1.2 m ditch cleaning bucket can also be fitted.

MAKE: TURNER (UK)   MODEL: Hydramower 25S

The Hydramower 25S is claimed to be the most advanced mower/hedgecutter available today. It can, as the name implies, reach 25 ft. (7.6 m) and can be fitted to special purpose vehicles as well as tractors. A telescopic second arm allows it to cut the far side of hedges, banks and ditches. Furthermore it cuts in an arc of 90 degrees to the left-hand side through 90 degrees to the right-hand side. The hydraulic system is 52 hp and it can be fitted to most well known makes of tractor in excess of 75 hp. Other attachments include a reed cutting bucket and a saw head.

MAKE: HARPLEY ENGINEERING (UK)
MODEL: GM Forest Scrubcutters

The GM Scrubcutter was developed for forest use to cope with the arduous conditions found in the thicket stage of plantation development. Hardened steel knives are mounted on a horizontal, cylindrical rotor and can rotate through 360 degrees when obstructions are encountered. The drive from the tractor is transmitted through a shaft fitted with a free wheel.

Spreaders

MAKE: BAMLETT (UK)   MODEL: Airjet

Bamlett pioneered the use of the pneumatic principle for improved accuracy of spreading and demand has led the company to produce wider 16 m, 18 m and 20 m booms. A wide range of materials can be applied including prills, granular compound, blended fertilizers, cereals, grass seeds, slug pellets, microgranules and urea. Accuracy is unaffected by cross winds, humidity levels or variations in particle size. To eliminate the problems of bounce, sway and yaw to which such wide booms would be susceptible, Bamletts developed in conjunction with the British Technology Group a combination of horizontal and vertical links to isolate the boom from the sharp movements of the tractor and hopper on uneven ground surfaces. The suspension system is self-centring so that the boom remains parallel to the ground even when on slopes. It also lifts for transport.

MAKE: ROGER (France)
MODEL: DPA Fertiliser Distributor

The Roger DPA is a pneumatic distributor which can spread microgranules, sulphates and granules evenly. The DPA—which stands for debit proportionnel a l'avancement—means that this French-made machine feeds matter at a rate directly proportional to forward rate. The operator can go slowly on a steep hill and quickly on a level field.

MAKE: VICON (Holland) MODEL: Vari-spreader

The Vari-spreader consists of a glass fibre reinforced polyester hopper and oscillating spout through which the fertilizer is spread. Models range in size from 275 litre capacity, which equates to about 5 bags of fertilizer, to 1500 litres, about 30 bags. The spreading width can be set between 6 and 12 metres.

MAKE: NORDSTEN (Denmark)   MODEL: Air-o-matic

The Nordsten Air-o-matic 12-metre fertilizer distributor has a 2-point quick hitch arrangement for easy and safe engagement, and the centre of gravity is close to the tractor, so therefore a smaller lifting capacity is required. As an option hydraulic folding of the booms can be operated from the driver's seat.

MAKE: MATCO VERBA (UK)
MODEL: Vertical Band Micro-granule Applicator

The model was designed to place chemicals where they belong, that is below the surface, in strategically selected vertical bands for carrots, parsnips and brassicas, in regular vertical bands for subsequent incorporation when treating potato land. The machine is used for controlling cystnematodes (eelworm), cabbage root fly, carrot fly and other pests.

MAKE: ECON ATKINSON'S (UK)
MODEL: Bettaspread Universal 820/970

The 820 and 970 manure spreaders have capacities of 8,000 and 10,000 kg respectively. The discharge is controlled by hydrostatic transmission to give variable speed and reverse. The heavy duty slatted moving floor gives high discharge rates, aided by chain driven twin shredding and distribution rotors. Heavy duty rear beaters to give a wider spread are an optional extra.

MAKE: MASSEY FERGUSON (Multi-national)
MODEL: MF 100 Slurry Tanker

The latest MF 100 tanker has a capacity of 5910 litres and it comes as standard with combine front tyres which carry the load at a low inflation pressure, thus minimizing rutting and soil compaction. The tanker has a remotely operated hydraulic gate valve and hydraulic power brakes. Spread width and density are variable.

MAKE: BIG A (USA)   MODEL: 4500 Spreader

Widely used in America and gaining popularity with contractors in eastern England, are high flotation 3- and 4-wheel self-propelled lime and fertilizer spreaders. This 16 tonne gross weight machine can cover 500 acres per day and has 4-wheel drive and steering. Note the high air cleaner intake to avoid dust.

MAKE: WEST (UK)   MODEL: Dual Spreader

The Mk III is a universal spreader for both solids and liquids, holding 5228 and 5910 litres according to model and size. The spreader has a third use as a silage feeder when the addition of a deflector plate converts the machine to a high output floor level forage feeder. The large capacity body is filled by fore-end loader, ramps or pumps. The feed auger moves the manure forward to spring plates which feed across to the spread rotor. The high speed spread rotor has channels which shred and spread the manure. A spring loaded tray is mounted under the spread rotor to assist the ejection of foreign bodies. A control door is adjusted hydraulically to give the feed rate required and a cam operated agitator assists in providing a continuous flow to the spread rotor.

MAKE: TWOSE (UK)
MODEL: Tandem Trailed Injection Machine

The Twose Tandem Trailed Injection Unit is mounted directly behind a tractor and linked via a supply hose to a tanker trailed behind a second tractor. It is a versatile machine and adaptable for those applications where there is a need to dispose of slurry, sludge and other liquid wastes compatible with agriculture but without the hazards of surface run off, odour and pollution. The liquid waste is drawn from the supply tanker by an integral pump and is injected beneath the ground by means of the Twose vibrating grassland tine assembly or standard arable injectors. The unit injects below the grassland with minimum surface disturbance to depths of 8 inches (203 mm); 2, 3 or 4 tines can be used to suit the power of the tractor and the ground conditions.

MAKE: TWOSE (UK)
MODEL: Twose 8000 Spreader Vehicle

The Twose 8000 Spreader Vehicle has a 192 hp Deutz V6 engined 4-wheel chassis/cab unit with a VM/Kongskilde 8-tonne spreader unit for fertilizer or lime. The unit is fully demountable and can be exchanged for the Twose injection equipment. The vehicle is extremely versatile, with a wide range of available optional attachments which allow many other uses of the unit during the whole year. The gearbox ensures synchronization of the distributing plates to give a uniform spreading pattern. Corrosion protection is a very high consideration with adjustment spindles and screws for the rubber tightening fillets in the fibre box made of stainless steel, whilst the conveyor pulleys, support pulleys and distributing plates are hot galvanized. The fertilizer box is made of fibre glass, which is corrosion resistant even to the most powerful fertilizers.

Ploughs

MAKE: RANSOMES (UK) MODEL: TSR300 Series

Reversible ploughs can make a big demand on the lift capacity and front end stability of tractors and so the 300 Series has been designed to overcome this. Compact design puts the weight of the plough well forward, close-up behind the tractor, thus making it suitable for tractors in the lower hp range. The headstock incorporates a double-acting hydraulic reversing mechanism, giving a smooth turnover and reliability; 2-, 3-, 4- and 5-row reversibles are available for tractors from 45 hp to 150 hp and feature one-man quick hitch attachment, sideshift and angling adjustment, and a variety of furrow widths.

MAKE: RANSOMES (UK)
MODEL: TSR300 Series Reversible Front Ploughs

The 'push-pull' makes it possible to plough up to 7 furrows with an 100 hp tractor and up to 9 furrows on 180 hp without the drawbacks of semi-mounting. With independent control the front plough can be raised out of work if the going gets tough.

MAKE: RANSOMES (UK)   MODEL: TSR300HD

The TSR300HD made by the British company, Ransomes, is a 5- and 6-furrow tractor-mounted reversible plough for large acreage ploughing and incorporates a unique headstock design to give extra lift clearance. It is intended to be used by tractors in the 120 hp to 200 hp range and disc coulters can be fitted.

75

MAKE: RANSOMES (UK)   MODEL: Disc Ploughs

Ransomes' fixed disc ploughs have proved their strength and dependability in some of the toughest farming territory in the world. Easily adjustable disc units allow the operator to choose the appropriate furrow width—narrow setting for hard land or a wide setting for coping with heavy surface trash. A range is offered from 3 to 5 furrows. Ransomes reversible disc ploughs give efficient, cost effective ploughing yet are simple to operate. With the furrows turned one way they leave the surface level meaning easier cultivation prior to drilling or planting. Reversing is semi-automatic and is achieved by a pull of a lever.

MAKE: KVERNELAND (Norway)   MODEL: LA

The Norwegian manufactured Kverneland LA is designed to cater for the smaller hp tractors with limited hydraulic lift capacity. The LA is a mounted light reversible plough made from high quality steel. It is available in 2- to 4-furrow versions with furrow widths of either 305 mm or 356 mm and an hydraulic turnover system.

MAKE: KVERNELAND (Norway)   MODEL: LB

The fully mounted reversible plough model LB with vari-width furrow adjustment is a new concept in plough design from Kverneland. The furrow width can be increased from 30 cm to 50 cm from the tractor seat by means of a linkage system. Vari-width ploughing allows the operator to suit different land conditions.

MAKE: KVERNELAND (Norway)   MODEL: D

The Kverneland 9–12 furrow trailed plough model D is built for the larger tractors and for effective ploughing of large acreages. A rugged square-beam provides the main frame of the plough and it is equipped with the Kverneland automatic reset system for non-stop ploughing in all conditions.

MAKE: KVERNELAND (Norway)   MODEL: MZ

The MZ is the model chosen by the winners of the

World Ploughing Championships. Not only designed for competition work, it is used by farmers for everyday farm ploughing. The MZ has a simple but strong construction. The Super models are fitted with a rectangular cross shaft and hydraulic front furrow width adjustment.

MAKE: MASSEY FERGUSON (Multi-national)
MODEL: MF 262

The MF 262 range of reversible ploughs embodies all the latest developments and covers 2- to 6-furrow models for tractor sizes up to 180 hp. The specification includes self-reset beams to allow non-stop ploughing irrespective of rocks or hidden obstructions. It has easily coupled hydraulics, a choice of headstocks and remote turnover from the driver's seat.

MAKE: NIEMEYER (West Germany)
MODEL: The Volly-Mat 03 Series

The Volly-Mat 03 Series features Vollymatic centre-line adjustment. This enables the operator to work out the correct line of draught in relation to the tractor rear wheel settings at the time. The result is a lower power requirement and less wear on both the tractor linkage and the plough.

MAKE: KRONE (West Germany)   MODEL: Mustang

Krone reversible ploughs of the Mustang series are available in 2 to 5 furrows and in working widths from 0.50 m to 2.50 m for all tractor sizes. The disc coulters shown here achieve a clean cut at the furrow edge. Skim coulters or manure and maize coulters of different types are also available.

Cultivators

MAKE: MASSEY FERGUSON (Multi-national)
MODEL: MF 280 Disc Harrow

With a weight per disc of 25 kg, the MF 280 is used as a medium weight finishing harrow allowing a seeding operation to follow speedily. The 457 or 508 mm diameter discs ensure that all the ground is fully tilled with cutaway discs available for the front gangs. Four sizes give working widths of 2.3, 2.7, 3.2 and 3.7 m.

MAKE: RANSOMES (UK)
MODEL: HR46A Trailed Disc Harrow

The HR46A range consists of 4 tough, massively

constructed harrows for performance and durability. Two hydraulically controlled wheels determine the working depth and 26-, 34- and 42-disc models are available for tractors in the 80–200 hp range. The two larger models are offered with hydraulic gang folding for ease of transport.

MAKE: NIEMEYER (West Germany)
MODEL: Rotary Power Harrows

These rotary power harrows have blade shaped tines and a selection of rear rollers for various operating conditions. The spiked roller with scraper, shown here, is used for medium to heavy soil and wet ground. The large number of spikes greatly increases the crumbling effect, whilst the other rollers are used for sandy soils.

MAKE: KVERNELAND (Norway)
MODEL: Soil Packers

Trailed behind the plough, soil packers are increasingly used for firming the soil and preventing moisture loss in a variety of land conditions. Hollow spaces between the soil clods are eliminated, large clods are chopped, crushed and packed. The narrow profile 700 mm and 900 mm cast rings penetrate deeply to root level for moisture retention, yet allow free drainage, while at the surface special 550 mm diameter notched cam rollers are designed to firm the seed bed for even sowing and germination. Soil packers are available with working widths from 1.05 m to 2.40 m, with a choice of single, double, off-set reversible, combination and front-mounted units. Features include cleaning chains, transport wheels and adjustable safety pick-up arms.

MAKE: RANSOMES (UK)   MODEL: C96 Subtiller

The C96 is designed to shatter the soil to a maximum depth of 406 mm for improved soil structure. It consists of narrow legs with reversible shins plus a point and wings and heavy duty disc coulters fitted in front of each unit to cut through surface vegetation. It is fitted here with a crumbler roll.

MAKE: CTM (UK)   MODEL: Tilthking

With a penetration depth of 255 mm, the Tilthking is used for preparing all seedbeds including potato land giving the deep tilth required for maximum yield. It can also be used on the autumn cultivation of stubble and pea ground. The welded construction steel frame carries 4 rows of deep cultivation tines, each of which is fully adjustable.

MAKE: KVERNELAND (Norway)
MODEL: Futura S Tine Cultivator

For gentle cultivation for the preparation of seed beds for beet and special crops, or for heavier work for dealing with deep-rooted weeds, the Futura is fitted with 4 different tine angle settings. The use of crumbler rollers leaves ground lightly compacted to ensure that the soil-moisture content is preserved.

MAKE: KONGSKILDE (Denmark)
MODEL: DC Seed Bed Cultivator

The DC range is designed for the smaller tractor with working widths from 1.7 to 3.4 m. Applications include aerating grassland, undercutting weed roots, uprooting seed weeds, thinning out winter crops and crumbling earth clods. Smooth side extensions to protect branches and stems enable the DC to be used under trees, bushes and along hedges and fences.

MAKE: RANSOMES (UK)
MODEL: C92 Heavy-duty Cultivator

The C92 3-bar cultivator is adjustable dependent on conditions and tractor power. Widths range from 2.45 m to 5.75 m. Tines available are the Terratine for deep cultivation such as stubble cleaning and pan busting, the Sweep tine for shallow work and the Pigtail and C spring tines, the last for cereal, pea and bean stubble.

MAKE: KONGSKILDE (Denmark)
MODEL: Vibro Beta

The Vibro Beta can be used for weed control in rape, mustard, beet, etc. and for mulching, aerating and incorporating manure and chemicals. The rolling shields protect leaves and roots and between 4 and 12 rows can be worked at a time at a speed of 2–5 mph. The stabilizing coulter provides steering and slides easily over stones.

MAKE: CTM (UK)   MODEL: Harrier

The Harrier seed covering harrow has been developed for high speed covering of broadcast cereals and incorporates features which allow for easy adaptation to suit individual conditions. Each standard 1250 mm long spring loaded tine bar can carry a maximum of 18 special profile lightweight spring tines. The Harrier is available in widths from 2.5 m to 12.5 m.

MAKE: HESTAIR (UK)
MODEL: WEBB 610 Rowcrop Hoe

The Rowcrop Hoe is offered in 4-, 5-, 6- and 7-row models and was developed to give a precision hoe producing a positive cutting action whilst avoiding excessive soil disturbance. These allow great accuracy when hoeing close to the growing crop and make the hoe suitable for areas susceptible to top 'blow', crusting and capping.

MAKE: HESTAIR (UK)
MODEL: Nicholson 625 Rowcleaner

The Rowcleaner is claimed to be the answer to inter-row cultivations in all rowcrops at all stages of crop growth. Crop protection shields float on their own independent parallel linkage for accurate ground following and inter-row widths down to 230 mm are obtainable from both tine and hoe modules, giving versatility for vegetables as well as sugar beat.

MAKE: RANSOMES (UK)
MODEL: C79 Multiple Row Ridger

The C79 is suitable for ridging potatoes, cotton, ground nuts, etc. The ridging bodies can be spaced from 609 mm upwards in 25 mm steps. They are adjustable for width of throw and can be used effectively for opening-up and moulding-up. Spring release attachments can be supplied to protect the bodies in rocky ground.

MAKE: REEKIE (UK)
MODEL: Three-row Auto-reset Ridger

The Reekie Ridger is robust and designed for non-stop high-speed ridging in the toughest conditions. The design of the Ridger beams allows the ploughs to lift out of work to clear buried obstacles, returning automatically to the working condition afterwards.

Stone Clearers

MAKE: KVERNELAND (Norway)
MODEL: Stone Rake

The Stone Rake made by the Norwegian firm of Kverneland is produced in 3 models: the 2000 with a working width of 2 m, the 3000 with 3 m and the 4000 with 4 m. These machines mechanize the work of stone picking and removal. They are mounted to the tractor's 3-point linkage and driven by the PTO. The tines rotate against the driving direction and with the Stone Rake working at an angle of 30 degrees stones are raked into a row on one side. The tines work up to a depth of 10 cm and with an operation speed of 2–3 mph, the 4000 has a capacity of 2.5 to 4.0 acres per hour, leaving the field cleared of dangerous and destructive stones.

MAKE: KVERNELAND (Norway)
MODEL: Stone Picker

The Kverneland Stone Picker can be used in conjunction with the Stone Rake to complete the operation of stone clearance. The principle of operation is that the stones and clods are gathered over the blade, which has a working width of 1650 mm, to the bar riddle. A conveyor then moves the stones and clods sideways and up a slotted, vibrating elevator which shakes off the soil. It then discharges them into a vehicle running alongside. Two sizes of riddle are available—for working with larger stones or smaller stones. The machine is mounted to a tractor's 3-point linkage and PTO. A 60 hp tractor is sufficient and the speed is kept low to minimize wear on chassis and bearings.

MAKE: GRIMME (West Germany)
MODEL: Tornado Stone and Clod Separator

The potato crop is particularly susceptible to damage during harvesting and the presence of even moderate amounts of stone in the ridges can reduce harvester output, increase tuber damage, and wear on the machinery. Furthermore, stones displace soil which could retain moisture and nutrients. Research has shown that depositing stones and clods in the bottom of the ridges between the plant rows is a cheaper and more effective way of overcoming the problem. This is known as stone windrowing and the Tornado is designed to carry out this operation. A smooth soil flow is achieved by multi-bladed and disc coulters. Heavy duty chains crush the clods and a cross conveyor deposits the stones to either left or right of the machine.

MAKE: REEKIE (UK)   MODEL: 300 SL Landscaper

The 300 SL Landscaper is used for the preparation of land to a high standard of tilth. Large amounts of stone, clod and other debris can be removed without the need for costly labour. It can clear ground at the rate of 1.85 acres per hour and can work in cultivated soil to a depth of 100 mm and pre-ridged land to 200 mm. The earth is picked up and passed over a series of webbed conveyors, with the separated soil cascading to the ground and the stones being discharged by a hydraulically operated loading elevator into a vehicle alongside. The machine is used by landscapers, forestry nurserymen, golf course and sportsfield contractors, road and pipeline contractors and for inland reclamation.

Rollers

MAKE: LAWRENCE EDWARDS (UK)
MODEL: DAL-BO

The DAL-BO hydraulic folding Cambridge rolls are frame mounted with hydraulically operated land rolls on a wheeled chassis, with a choice of plain or serrated rings. They are used for breaking up the heaviest soils and providing an even, compact seedbed, which results in improved moisture retention and faster germination. Working widths from 4 m to 10 m are available.

MAKE: MICHAEL MOORE (UK)
MODEL: Folding Roll

The Michael Moore Folding Roll convertor kit consists of a complete steel box section frame assembly which lifts hydraulically the outer rolls for transporting. It has a working width of between 4.87 m and 7.31 m and each kit is built individually to customer specification. A full range of rings, shafts, etc., is available.

SOWING

After preparing the land the farmer sows the seeds of whatever he has decided to grow and here we consider the variety of machines for doing this.

The broadcaster is less popular today and farmers prefer a seed drill which is towed behind the tractor and is often over 6 metres wide. It cuts a number of parallel grooves in the ground, drops a continuous supply of seeds into each groove and then covers them. Rate and depth may be altered to suit the crop and some machines can add fertilizer to the sown seed.

Where ploughing may not have taken place and only a little cultivation has been carried out, a direct drill is used. This works in the same way but is more robust and has heavy coulters for cutting into the ground.

Crops such as cabbage, lettuce and beet need room to develop and ideally are planted at regular intervals. For this the farmer uses a precision drill which plants a single seed per row at specified distances.

Seed potatoes require careful handling and selection during planting. Automatic machines are available but, being complicated, they are expensive. So most farmers use a machine that is manned. The machine places the seed potatoes into furrows, formed in advance by a ridging plough, and covers them over.

To assist his crop in competing with weeds and combating disease and pests, the farmer will probably spray his crop from time to time whilst it is growing. This is done with sprayers attached to the tractor. The wider they are the less he will damage his crop by driving through it. Depending on the width of his sprayer the farmer will have first marked out his field at intervals and will always drive up the same parallel 'tramlines' so that soil compaction and crop damage are kept to a minimum.

Irrigation equipment may be used during excessively long dry spells to water the crop.

Drills

MAKE: BAMLETT (UK)   MODEL: CD 4.0 m Drill

Bamlett's patented feed unit precisely meters almost any combination of seed and fertilizer to ensure the sowing rate required. Even spacing in the row is maintained by straight sided coulter tubes to prevent any interruption of flow. Special coulter springs and positive coulter pressure ensure an even sowing depth across the drill.

MAKE: VICON (Holland)
MODEL: Supaseeder Seed Drill LZ401

The Supaseeder is a pneumatic seeder designed to give the accuracy and versatility required for the modern trends in cereal and other crop cultivation. The basic design allows versions of different row spacings to be supplied and the distribution system can deal with small seeds or large. Seed rate is variable between 1 and 140 kg per acre.

MAKE: HESTAIR (UK)   MODEL: Bettinson TC4

The TC4 has low ground pressure tyres, an extra large quick fill hopper, calibration cassettes to control the exact rates of seed application and metering rollers made from soft urethane to avoid harmful bruising of seeds. This British made machine also features automatic depth control, a choice of coulters and double coulter springs for high speed drilling.

MAKE: WESTMAC FIONA (Denmark)
MODEL: SF 85 Drill

Fiona's special peg type sowing wheels can cope with virtually all kinds of seed and granular fertilizers including very fine seeds such as alfalfa, clover, carrots and rape, which are usually sown in small quantities per acre. A number of hard nylon components are used in the machine and ensure superior corrosion resistance and reduced maintenance.

MAKE: MASSEY FERGUSON (Multi-national)
MODEL: MF30

Accuracy of planting is achieved in two ways with

the MF30. Firstly, the metering units measure the exact quantity of seed required and, secondly, a hydraulic ram applies pressure through long coulter springs to push the coulters into the ground. It can sow anything from tick beans to mustard seed, including cereals covered with sticky seed dressings.

MAKE: HESTAIR (UK)   MODEL: Stanhay S981

The S981 is a versatile single line drill capable of drilling a wide variety of crops at row widths 230 mm upwards and is available with 4 to 18 row units. The hydraulic cab-operated folding yoke bar will accommodate up to 12 rows; and for short headland work, half the drill can be held vertical whilst the other half works.

Planters

MAKE: SMALLFORD (UK)   MODEL: Setrite

The Setrite gives precision spacing from 152 mm to 610 mm at row widths between 660 mm and 914 mm. Rubber cups convey seed from the metering unit to the ground. There is provision for 2 operators, who ensure good planting by rectification as required. A planting speed of $\frac{3}{4}$ mph is possible, and fertilizer and bulb planting attachments are offered.

MAKE: UNDERHAUGS RANSOMES (Norway)
MODEL: Faun Automatic Potato Planters

These planters are available in 2-row and 4-row versions. In a normal working day the 2-row can plant 10 acres (4 hectares) and the 4-row double that amount. Both can be equipped with a fertilizer attachment and an insecticide applicator. Row width and depth can be adjusted and either ridging shovels or disc coverers are available.

MAKE: REEKIE (UK)
MODEL: Automatic Potato Planter

The Reekie is a robust, high capacity machine claimed to have many advantages over existing planters. A 760 kg hopper speeds up bulk loading and similarly the optional fertilizer attachment has a capacity of 304 kg. Broad based ploughs fitted with ridge finishing chains form full ridges with uniform seed cover; and the toothed planting belt gives accurate spacing.

Sprayers

MAKE: VICON (Holland)
MODEL: Precision Sprayers

   Vicon sprayers are manufactured as tractor-mounted models from 630 to 1300 litres capacity and trailed machines of 2300 and 3600 litres capacity. The eight different models are available with a choice of booms, pumps and options. The close-coupled spin moulded polyethylene tanks keep the weight of the spray liquid well forward to assist tractor stability. A single trapezium stabilization system is fitted as standard to these sprayers and a double trapezium is available as an option providing full automatic boom stabilization. The 2-position automatic system can be set for flat land work maintaining a horizontal boom even if the tractor runs in a rut. The hillside setting automatically maintains the boom at the angle of the incline. The chemical filling probe can suck chemicals straight from the can.

MAKE: ETS MATROT (France)   MODEL: Mobilcord

The Mobilcord is claimed to be a most efficient machine for treating sugar beet weeds, bolters and others. A reservoir is filled with herbicide and feeds an impregnation tank. Two endless ropes are then passed through this tank and become impregnated. These ropes then slide over the leaves and stems, thus applying the herbicide.

MAKE: CHAVIOT (UK)   MODEL: 801

The Chaviot has been purpose designed to allow easy access for crop treatment all through the year, even in the most difficult soil conditions. Unlike a tractor's, the Chaviot's load is positioned between the front and rear axles and so the weight is distributed between them. Most arable land is very wet and will not support heavily loaded tyres from October to March, but increasing the tyre width will reduce the ground pressure and result in less damage. The Chaviot has 355 mm wide tyres, will work in tramlines at any spacing from 1·5 m to 1·8 m and will, depending on payload, exert only 4 psi. It is designed for operators spraying up to 10,000 acres a year, has power steering and a top speed of 30 mph.

MAKE: SANDS AGRICULTURAL MACHINERY (UK)
MODEL: Forward Control Sprayer

Based on the well-proven Case 1494 Skid Unit of 84 hp the SAM has Hydrostatic power steering, hydraulic clutch and brakes and 12 forward speeds. It has a 2000 litre capacity tank and its forward position gives the operator maximum control for fast accurate spraying. The Hydro-Mechanical boom suspension is terrain following.

MAKE: MOTESKA SPRAYERS (UK)
MODEL: MF-1250 Spraying Kit

Moteska manufacture a wide range of spraying equipment for use with a variety of tractors and power units. This kit is specifically designed for the Massey Ferguson MF-1250 and MF-1200 tractors and has a 2000 litre capacity fibreglass tank. Booms are available from 12 to 24 metres in width and have full hydraulic control of height, opening/closing, contouring with full breakback system, centrifugal force dampers on both wings, single or double spraylines with colour coded quick-change nozzle caps and diaphragm check valves. Systems are available for both liquid and suspension fertilizers. There are 5-valve electric controls in the cab with pressure compensation. If air-control is required, a compressor and air-valves may be fitted. The pump is a 6-cylinder piston/diaphragm type.

MAKE: MOTESKA SPRAYERS (UK)
MODEL: Mercedes MB-Trac Spraying Kit

The Moteska kit for the MB-Trac is largely similar to that for MF tractors. Additionally, though, it features a close-coupled 2-wheel bogie to carry the boom, thus reducing the loading upon the back of the MB-Trac. The 2000-litre tank is mounted on the tractor's rear platform and the pump is driven by the rear PTO.

Irrigator

MAKE: PERROT (West Germany)   MODEL: Peromat

The Perrot hose reel irrigator not only distributes clean water but also effluent, sludge and slurry. Pipe lengths up to 500 m and diameters from 90 mm to 125 mm are available. The drive is implemented via an A-turbine with special Perrot impeller. A precise irrigation is given due to the system consisting of the bypass layer compensating steering.

HARVESTING

Harvesting is basically gathering or picking the crop that you have grown. As there are a great many different types of crop, a wide variety of harvesters are available. These vary in complexity depending on the difficulty of picking a crop. Most fruit harvesting, for example, is still done by hand.

The combine harvester, which harvests seed crops, is so called because it 'combines' what used to be two individual operations, namely, the cutting and the threshing. Threshing is the separation of the seed from the chaff, husk or pod. The crop is pulled by the reel over cutting blades, compressed and transported into the machine by the auger, carried through a system usually consisting of threshing rollers and sieves, and finally the grain is stored in a tank and the debris is cast out of the rear. Straw choppers can then be employed to cut and distribute this debris for eventual ploughing in.

There are specialist harvesters for peas and beans, fruit, cane and vegetables, even aquatic plants, a selection of which are shown. Some, of course, are more appropriate to particular parts of the world than others.

Sugar beet is a deep-rooted crop and requires sophisticated equipment to harvest it. Most potato pickers expose the potatoes and lift them onto the machine for human pickers to complete the task of selection.

There are a wide variety of mowers for cutting green foliage. Some are fitted with conditioners which bruise or crimp the crop to allow moisture to escape so that it dries quickly to make hay. Rotary tedders and rakes assist this drying process by spreading and turning the crop. The square balers, which collect, compress and tie bales, have been supplemented more recently by round balers which make a large roll.

If the farmer chooses to make silage, he can use a forage harvester. This may cut the crop or simply pick-up the pre-cut swathe and chop the foliage. It then blows it into a trailer by means of a spout. Alternatively, the cut crop whilst still fresh and green may be gathered by a round baler and the resultant bale be placed in a large black polythene bag to preserve it.

Combine harvesters

MAKE: SPERRY NEW HOLLAND (Multi-national)
MODEL: TF

The TF combines feature a large diameter 6-reel bar for picking up the crop and carrying it from the knife to the auger. The speed of this reel is controlled electrically by a switch in the cab. Various widths of headers are available from 4.75 m to 6.70 m, and 5-, 6-, or 8-row maize headers can be supplied with the TF. The operator can pre-set ground pressure to give automatic header compensation to allow for irregularities in the terrain and to avoid bulldozing. The TF 42 is available in manual and hydrostatic versions and is powered by a 180 hp engine whilst the TF 44 has hydrostatic transmission as standard and a 216 hp power plant. The TF 42 has a grain store tank of 6340 litres and the TF 44 a capacity of 7040 litres. The rapid unloading auger moves 70 litres a second and empties the TF 44 in just $1\frac{1}{2}$ minutes.

MAKE: JOHN DEERE (USA)
MODEL: 1055 Combine

The 1055 is a mid-sized 4-walker combine. The 3000 litre grain tank is emptied by the swivel type auger which can be swung out electrically to an angle of 90 degrees. The 6-cylinder John Deere diesel produces 105 hp with a displacement of 5.9 litres. The threshing cylinder is claimed to be the largest in its class with 8 rasp bars. In good crop conditions more than 90 per cent of the grain separation takes place here. Opposed action cleaners prevent clogging, with the chaffer and grain pan moving one way and the sieve the other. More than 20 access doors aid servicing and the range of attachments includes a straw chopper, a straw spreader, a platform trailer and a 4-row maize header with low profile gathering snouts that even pick up flattened stalks.

MAKE: JOHN DEERE (USA)   MODEL: 1075

The 1075 has a turbocharged 5880 cc engine developing 150 hp and ample torque to maintain constant cylinder speed in rolling hills and run a straw chopper in long, heavy straw. Either Posi-Torq drive which transfers engine power through a variable speed control to the 4-speed transmission and the front wheel drive or Hydro 4 hydrostatic drive which provides instant forward/reverse and speed control through 4 torque ranges can be supplied. A 6-bar metal reel picks up down crops in front of the cutter bar and sweeps the cut material into the feed auger. Flighting on the auger pinches the crop, pulling it to the centre of the table where it is swept into the feeder house. The cutter knife makes 940 cuts per minute.

MAKE: JOHN DEERE (USA)
MODEL: 1085 Combine

Similar in many ways to the 1075, the 1085 Combine has a turbocharged 7643 cc power plant which produces 170 hp on the standard Posi-Torq model and 195 hp on the Hydro 4 optional transmission. There is no clutch with the Hydro 4, just a control lever giving forward and reverse, which saves time with entangled down crops when frequent reversing is required. A cab designed for good visibility, ease of control and comfort is a feature of the John Deere combines. An 'information centre' gives the level of grain in the tank, and has a low shaft speed monitor, a performance monitor dial, a relative forward speed indicator, an electric stubble height indicator and an accumulator pressure gauge. The performance monitor warns the operator of overloading or under-capacity.

MAKE: JOHN DEERE (USA)
MODEL: 1068H Sidehill Combine

The John Deere 1068H is designed to be an economical answer to the problems of harvesting on a slope. Automatic side-to-side levelling maintains harvesting efficiency on slopes as steep as a 12 degree gradient. The 1068H levelling system keeps the separation and cleaning functions level for maximum efficiency and allows higher ground speeds. The cutting platform and rear wheels pivot, while the feederhouse opening remains constant regardless of the platform angle. The makers claim that farmers will enjoy considerably increased productivity compared to flat land combines used on slopes without the cost of special expensive hillside machines. With safety in mind, heavy duty disc brakes are mounted next to the wheels and in the event of hydraulic pressure dropping, the levelling system locks in position.

MAKE: SHELBOURNE REYNOLDS (UK)
MODEL: The Self-Propelled Swather

The problem with rape and many seed crops is that if left to get too ripe the pods shatter before they enter the combine and the seeds are lost. Many farmers therefore cut it earlier and let it dry in the field (swathing). The combine is then able to pick up the dried rape and thresh it with less wastage. The Shelbourne Reynolds Self-propelled Swather was designed for this purpose. The variable speed 6-bar reel and bed and cutter bar cut the crop quickly and leave it neatly spread to allow even ripening, and in a continuous swath for optimum combine performance. The tractor unit is based on the Fortschritt E301 equipped with a rugged 60 hp engine. It has 2 forward and 1 reverse gears.

MAKE: SHELBOURNE REYNOLDS (UK)
MODEL: Pick-up Header

After the seed crop has been pre-cut, the cut swaths require extreme care when being lifted. With the Pick-up Header, which can be attached to virtually every make of combine, the crop is gently lifted onto the combine table, feeding the combine with dry material. It can harvest both seeds and cereals and allows a faster speed to be achieved.

MAKE: CLAAS (West Germany)
MODEL: Dominator 96

The German built Claas 96 is fitted with a 6-cylinder

diesel engine which produces 150 hp and drives through a manual transmission with 3 forward and 1 reverse gear. Hydrostatic transmission and 4-wheel drive are available. The cutter bar assists the harvesting of laid crop smoothly and the two 3-part crop lifters are mounted to allow independent flotation. The Claas intensive separation system is made up of 2 parts. There are long straw walkers, slatted sections with 4 steps and 2 cranks fitted with movement controlled tines. Claas harvesters can be used not only for cereals such as wheat, rye, barley and oats, but also for pulse and oil seed crops such as beans, soya beans, field beans, lucerne, flax and rape, plus grass, clover, beet seeds, sunflowers, millet, sorghum, and sesame.

MAKE: CLAAS (West Germany)
MODEL: Dominator 114CS

The Dominator 114CS is a large-scale combine with the Claas 'Cylinder System' for separating the straw from the grain. From the cutter bar, which it is claimed can separate the heaviest crop and lodged straw from green growth, and which can be varied in speed of operation from 14 to 55 rpm, the crop passes to the thresher. The thresher is equipped with heavy rasp bars and 6 drum plates. From here the crop is forced through a series of separate cylinders and separation concaves fitted beneath the cylinders. Claas claim this system to be more efficient than walkers and allows hillside working. The 114CS is driven by a Mercedes 220 hp engine with hydrostatic ground speed transmission. The 114CS has a grain tank capacity of 6000 litres which can be emptied in around a minute.

MAKE: FIATAGRI (Italy)   MODEL: Laverda 3850

The Laverda 3850 manufactured by the Fiatagri group, is the second largest of the 3000 series combines. It is intended for big cereal farms and contractors. Fiatagri claim particularly effective cleaning with the long stepped surface of the grain pan improving selection of the material and evening out the flow of material to the sieves. The sieve area coupled with a high fan, whose intake is shielded to prevent intake of chaff, ensures fast expulsion of chaff and waste from the top sieve. The divided fan is speed controlled by a variator and adjustable air stream deflectors direct the flow. The Laverda 3850 is powered by a Fiat turbocharged 6-cylinder which produces 175 hp. The table auger, together with the feed roller and straw elevator, are reversible in case of blockage.

MAKE: MASSEY FERGUSON (Multi-national)
MODEL: MF 8 Plot Combine

The MF 8 is a plot combine developed to work in areas where a large number of small plots are harvested, either by plant breeding institutes, the agrochemical industry, research stations and others. It was designed and developed to avoid cross fertilization and crop contamination. It is easy to clean with a rubber belt conveyor to cylinder as opposed to chains, sprockets and elevator bars where seeds can get lodged or damaged. The compact dimensions, excellent manoeuvrability and hydrostatic transmission ensure easy operation in small plots. The MF 8 is available in either tanker or bagger versions and is powered by a Perkins engine which develops some 55 hp. The grain tank has a capacity of 0.7 cubic metres or 19 bushels.

MAKE: MASSEY FERGUSON (Multi-national)
MODEL: MF 24

The range of MF Hydro's consists of 4 combines, the MF 24, 27, 29 and 31. The MF 24 is the smallest of the range but incorporates the same advanced specification of the larger models. It is powered by a 101 hp Perkins 6-cylinder diesel and has a 1·1 m wide cylinder. Cuttings of 3·2 m or 3·65 m widths are available.

MAKE: MASSEY FERGUSON (Multi-national)
MODEL: MF 31

Top of the Massey Ferguson range is the MF 31. It is powered by a 153 hp turbocharged Perkins with charge cooling, and takes cutting tables up to 4·88 m. The MF 27, 29 and 31 models feature the Unicontrol computer which monitors all functions from fuel level to actual time in work and gives advance warning of malfunctions.

MAKE: DEUTZ-FAHR (West Germany)
MODEL: M2680

The Deutz-Fahr M2680 has a cutting width depending on choice—3 m, 3.60 m or 4.20 m. The machine has a heavy duty threshing drum, high ribbed grain pan and straw walker units. It is driven by an air cooled 6128 cc 6-cylinder, 121 hp diesel of their own manufacture. The 3-speed transmission enables the operator to vary his speed from $\frac{1}{2}$–2 mph in first to 12 mph in third for road travel. The Commander cab is iso-mounted, free of vibration and very quiet with effective sound proofing. Air conditioning is standard on the de luxe models and good visibility allows the driver to watch the crop and operation clearly. The Agrotronic in-cab information system monitors up to 21 key functions and gives visual and acoustic signals that help in maximizing output.

MAKE: FORTSCHRITT (East Germany)
MODEL: E512

The E512 can be fitted with cutters of either 4.20 m or 5.70 m of the spring balanced type, being held in position by 2 hydraulic cylinders. It has a larger than average threshing cylinder and its speed is infinitely variable. Emptying of the grain bin may be carried out whilst still harvesting, thus saving time. The loss of grain during harvesting is, in general, between 0.10 and 0.37 per cent. The E512 can be used for harvesting more than 70 different crops, including clover, alfalfa, peas, beans, tares, lupins, beets, serradella, carrots, spinach, poppy, caraway and others. There is a specialized rice threshing unit available as are 4-row and 6-row corn pickers and a sunflower cutting unit. These harvesters, and East German agricultural equipment in general, are marketed under the name Fortschritt.

MAKE: MASSEY FERGUSON (Multi-national)
MODEL: 860

The Massey Ferguson 860 is powered by a Perkins AT6 4544 cc power plant which yields 160 hp and drives through a hydrostatic transmission with a 4-range constant gearbox. It has a cutter bar width of 4.8 m, with 2 serrated knives working at 1200 strokes per minute. The crop elevator has 6 rotating paddles, the cylinder has 8 rasp bars, and there are 6 walkers.

Straw choppers

MAKE: RANSOMES (UK)
MODEL: BNG 230 Straw Chopper

Ransomes' compact, tractor mounted straw chopper is built to deal with the largest straw swaths left by the combines. The short chop length is achieved by two sets of knives in combination with straight flails attached to the rotor shaft driven at a maximum speed of 2025 rpm. Deflectors attached to the rear hood of the machine combine with the 'fan action' of the flail spacers to ensure a wide spread pattern. Working height is controlled by the rear mounted wheels and skids. The headstock can be re-positioned to allow the machine to be offset from the tractor and a pivoting link location enables the machine to follow the undulations of the ground. Alternative flails can be fitted for cutting grass and other crop residues, such as kale and maize stalks.

MAKE: KIDD (UK) MODEL: Straw Chopper

There are two main criteria for a straw chopper to satisfy. First it must chop short enough so that the following cultivations are completely successful; and, secondly, the straw that is buried with plough, or incorporated, must decompose in the shortest possible time. Therefore a good short chop evenly spread satisfies these objectives and this is what the Kidd straw chopper is designed to achieve. It has a 2 m wide pick-up to deal with swath straw from combine headers up to 5 m. Chopped straw can be spread from 2 m up to 5 m wide depending on weather conditions.

MAKE: TAARUP (Denmark) MODEL: SKT 1500 & 2100

The two Taarup machines, the model numbers denote the cutting widths, are designed for the user to carry out a variety of field operations including tedding, windrowing, straw cutting and spreading, and maize stalk cutting and spreading. The ploughing down of straw, maize stalks, potato haulm, beet tops or surface trash then becomes a simpler operation, the material being easily buried and thereby enriching the humus content of the soil. The SKT 1500 is closely coupled behind the tractor and is mounted on the normal 3-point mounting. It is supplied with skids for height adjustment and requires little maintenance. The SKT 2100 is like the smaller model but is displaced to the right-hand side and has two support wheels.

MAKE: WEST (UK)   MODEL: Meteor Straw Chopper

This British machine was basically designed for cubicle bedding. It is driven from the tractor's PTO via a bevel gearbox. The chopping action is carried out through 45 serrated fixed blades and 36 plain moving blades fixed to the rotating table. The rear is lowered hydraulically for loading on up to 1·5 m diameter bales.

Pea harvesters

MAKE: FMC (UK)   MODEL: 879 Long Drum

The FMC Long Drum pea harvester's high capacity enables a farmer to use fewer machines to harvest his crop. This and the manufacturer's claims of less servicing, less maintenance and less labour are the advantages of the long drum machine. The extended threshing drum 1·4 m longer than the standard FMC machines, increases the threshing and recovery area by 38 per cent to make full use of FMC's 5-beater planetary threshing system. The picking reel has variable speed drive, automatic ground pressure control and a full-width driven ground roller. The power pack on this harvester is a 273 hp Deutz V8 driving through 4-wheel hydrostatic transmission, plus an automatic levelling system. To ensure long periods of uninterrupted working, it has a 470 litres fuel tank.

MAKE: FMC (UK)   MODEL: 679 Range

FMC have developed a range of pea and broad bean harvesting machines to suit a variety of operating conditions. Two power options are available—either a Deutz 6-cylinder turbocharged air cooled unit which develops 180 hp or a 214 hp V8 Deutz. Four-wheel hydrostatic drive is standard on the V8 machine and is an option on the smaller model. Picking heads of 2.8, 3.2 and 3.4 metres widths will pick peas in any direction, in wet or dry conditions, in one pass. Spring tines comb the pods off the vine in twice-over action leaving the plant still rooted in the ground. The FMC patented 5-beater planetary threshing system is said to be unique. Two inclined aprons and a primary fan clean the threshed peas.

MAKE: SHELBOURNE REYNOLDS (UK)
MODEL: SB 8000 Turbo

The Shelbourne Reynolds SB 8000 Turbo pea and broad bean harvester enables one man to harvest 2½ acres per hour. Short-strawed crops can be recovered up to 50 per cent faster than by using traditional viners. Automatic levelling copes with most slopes and ensures that more of the crop is gathered. The 3.2 m picking reel takes pods direct from the plant without pre-cutting. Inside the threshing chamber, multi-blade beaters and stripper drums give faster threshing and a cleaner crop. A 4-stage cleaning system removes waste material and the 1¼ tonne storage hopper can be tipped out on the move. An all-weather panoramic cab, control consoles and night working lights are supplied. This British built machine is powered by a water-cooled turbocharged 8-cylinder 245 hp Perkins diesel.

Fruit harvester

MAKE: SMALLFORD (UK)   MODEL: Multi

The Smallford Multi harvesting machine consists of a basic chassis which is attached to a Case International tractor. This chassis with various attachments and variations can be used for harvesting grapes, strawberries, red and black currants and gooseberries. For strawberry harvesting a double reciprocating cutter bar, over which a combine type header unit rotates, cuts below the clusters and leaves which have already been lifted by spring tine 'fingers' in front of the blades. For grapes, flexible tines shake off individual grapes which then fall onto spring-loaded 'fishplates' wrapped around the vines. As the plates move in and out, fruit is brushed onto conveyors and thence backwards for leaf separation. Gooseberries, red and black currants are harvested in a similar way. Bulk containers are carried at the rear and the five specialized harvester and sprayer units all fit the basic chassis.

Cane harvesters

MAKE: CARIB BRUFF (UK)   MODEL: Cane Cutter

The machine base cuts the cane at ground level leaving no stubble and strips most of the trash free from the cane stalks which are left in an orderly windrow. Field workers then pull the canes from the windrows, remove the tops, and pile them in the usual way, ready for loading.

MAKE: CATERPILLAR (USA)   MODEL: Oahu Sugar

To remove the cut cane from the fields some major producers use special haul units based on crawler tractors. In this case in Hawaii, the basis is a Caterpillar with all the controls moved forward to an offset cab. When the trailer reaches the road it is reconnected to a truck for transfer to the sugar extraction mills.

Vegetable harvesters

MAKE: FABCO (USA)   MODEL: Lettuce Harvester

The Fabco lettuce harvester is powered by a Detroit

4-53 turbocharged 2-stroke diesel. It features all-wheel drive for sticky conditions and has 30 speeds provided by a combination of main gearbox, 3-speed auxiliary and 2-speed transfer box. Thus it can travel at 1 mph whilst being loaded in wet lettuce fields and 55 mph on its way to market.

MAKE: DAVID THOMAS (UK)
MODEL: Turnip & Swede Harvester

Operated from the normal tractor hydraulics, the hydraulically driven topper and lifting mechanism can be used by one man. It can fill trailers on the headland or can tip directly into a clamp. The tractor and machine travel on ground already harvested which eliminates any damage to the crop by the tractor or trailer wheels.

MAKE: HARPLEY ENGINEERING (UK)
MODEL: CTM Veg-Plough

The CTM Veg-Plough is suited to both large and small growers who require a good sample with minimum damage. The single row lifter, which is driven off the tractor's PTO, is adjustable from 460–560 mm row widths and with various share options will lift a variety of crops e.g. parsnips, carrots, turnips and swedes. An inline hydraulic topper, powered by the tractor's hydraulic system, tops the crop and deposits the leaf away from the row being lifted. The crop is lifted by a pair of fixed shares set between large discs which cut the ground and guide the roots onto the lifting web, from where they are transferred to the cross conveyor and then discharged in rows on the surface for hand picking and sorting. A 50–75 hp tractor is required.

Beet

MAKE: HARPLEY ENGINEERING (UK)
MODEL: CTM Forager

This forager is a robustly constructed, easily manoeuvrable machine for the collection of sugar beet tops and pea haulm for silage making or direct feeding. Driven from a tractor PTO with a minimum power of

35 hp, it can deliver the crop to a rear trailer or via an elevator into a trailer towed alongside.

MAKE: TODD (UK)   MODEL: Beet Cleaner Loader

The Todd Beet Cleaner Loader cleans the crop at a rate of 120 tonnes per hour, which is fast enough to keep most loading shovels working hard. It has a heavy duty Lister diesel engine and a large capacity 2·12 cubic metres hopper, with an optional extension to increase to 3·4 cubic metres capacity for use with larger loading shovels.

MAKE: STANDEN (UK)   MODEL: Rapide Mk. 3A

Designed for the farmer with a beet contract of up to 70 acres, the trailed Rapide has a big diameter ground speed driven feeler-wheel, which tops one row ahead of the lifting wheels, ensuring the top of the knife cuts precisely. A spring-loaded disc provides a channel for the knife arm to follow and the tops are whisked away by a rubber flipper to leave the roots for lifting. Traditional lifting wheels ease the beet from the ground, cutting through surface trash and lifting the minimum of soil. A set of rubber star wheels feeds the beet onto the trash extractor web, which in turn ejects unwanted material over the rear of the harvester. With a 1·8 tonnes capacity tank one man can operate the machine in all but the largest fields.

MAKE: MOREAU (France)
MODEL: GR Series Self-propelled Beet Harvesters

The Moreau self-propelled beet harvesters are driven by a turbocharged, direct injection 6-cylinder engine. A 570 litre fuel tank allows many hours of work before having to stop to refuel. Large diameter radial ply pneumatic tyres considerably improve the grip and the balance of the machine on wet, heavy land and on slopes. The short wheelbase (420 cm) enables the machine to have a modest turning circle. It is fitted with hydrostatic transmission with a single lever allowing fingertip adjustment of the speed to suit working conditions. The cab has large tinted glass windows for good visibility and the angle of the windscreen prevents sun nuisance. It is possible to install 18 combinations of beet harvesting equipment to the basic GR frame. A direct loading elevator and a holding tank are also available options.

Aquatic harvester

MAKE: AQUAMARINE (Canada)
MODEL: H7-400 Aquatic Plant Harvester

The Canadian company of Aquamarine produces a full range of harvesters for water management. They are used for plant clearance from, and restoration of, small ponds, lakes, canals and rivers. The H7-400 is a mid-range, powerful, heavy duty, professional machine for the control of medium to large weed beds. It has a 215 cm cutting width with a 10 cm zinc plated, serrated knife system and the suspended pivoting harvesting head is well protected against damage from underwater hazards. The elevated control bridge has a combination of foot and manual hydraulic controls and full instrumentation. The diesel power unit is control-bridge mounted for maximum protection against condensation and is easily accessible. The harvester's transport trailer doubles as a conveyor for dumping aquatic plant material and is bi-directional, being powered by its own engine.

Potato harvesters

MAKE: GRIMME (West Germany)   MODEL: Crusader

The Crusader uses 2 revolving brush belts to sweep the crop from the cross spiked bands giving a large area to separate the crop from soils with heavy stone content. Flexibility of control is given by 3 speeds in the gearbox, 2-speed drive haulm elevator and variable speed hydraulic drives to separator and picking off area.

MAKE: GRIMME (West Germany)
MODEL: Q and QC Continental

These 2-row potato harvesters are claimed to be **8** harvesters in one. Being modular they can be changed to suit a wide variety of harvesting conditions. Each module is designed to fit in place of the third web section to tune the harvester into particular soil conditions which can be found from district to district. The QC has a large picking area and two platforms allow the machine to be staffed with 4 pickers. The up and over elevator carries the potatoes from the main web to the crop inspection area. An onion harvesting attachment is also available.

MAKE: FORTSCHRITT (East Germany)
MODEL: Weimar Qualitat 1

The Qualitat 1 is a single-row big capacity potato harvester designed to meet the requirements of the small to medium-sized growers. It is available either as a bunker or bagger model and can be fitted with either a rubber finger belt and brush separator for the removal of stones or Multisep separator for the removal of clods and small flat stones.

MAKE: UNDERHAUGS/RANSOMES (Norway)
MODEL: Superfaun

The Superfaun potato digger is mounted to a tractor by means of the 3-point fixing. It is offset to lift the ridge outside the tractor to eliminate wheel damage to the crop. In addition to the lifting share, the unit incorporates the digging wheel with 4 rubber protected digging tines and a powered guide disc. The digging wheel and tines break down the ridge and, with the help of the guide disc, the broken down ridge is delivered direct on to the inside of the first elevator belt, which runs behind and below the share. Most of the haulm and trash is discharged at the top of the first conveyor. The haulm is carried under the deflector, caught by the powered haulm rollers and then discharged. The sorting conveyor can be operated at 2 speeds to suit the pickers.

Mowers

MAKE: JOHN DEERE (USA)
MODEL: 1315 Mower Conditioner

The John Deere 1315 uses a combination of rotary cutting and impeller conditioning and is one of the smaller mowers in the range with a cutting width of 2 m. The 1315 works at twice the speed of sickle-knife/crusher-roll machines. It will cut all grasses including Italian ryegrass and legumes like lucerne or thick clovers.

MAKE: JOHN DEERE (USA)
MODEL: 1327 Mower Conditioner

The 1327 is similar to the 1315 but has a 2.8 m width of cut. The conditioning of the cut grass is achieved by the speed differential of the crop passing between the conditioning hood and the tines of the impeller. The crop dries more quickly because the waxy outer coatings of the stems are scuffed.

MAKE: VICON (Holland)
MODEL: CM 135, 165, 216 & 240 Disc Mowers

Vicon disc mowers are manufactured in 4 widths from 1·35 m to 2·40 m and will cut heavy standing grasses and laid, tangled crops. Triangular discs with 3 blades rotate at 3000 rpm and alternate discs contra-rotate to leave the swath neatly and evenly distributed to aid drying. Equipped with a hydraulic cylinder they can operate at 45 degrees.

MAKE: VICON (Holland)
MODEL: KM 241, 281 & 321

The Vicon range of mower conditioners has working widths of 2·4 m, 2·9 m and 3·2 m. The grass is cut by the disc cutter bar and conditioned by crimping over nylon rollers. The unusual thing about this range is the full swivel hitch which allows the mower to turn a square corner without reversing and driving over previously cut crop.

MAKE: MASSEY FERGUSON (Multi-national)
MODEL: MF 70

Historically, rotary mowers have either been bottom

drive with bottom support or top drive with top support. Both had advantages and disadvantages, so Massey Ferguson produced the MF 70 with the rotors driven from the top and supported at the bottom. Conditioning is carried out by beater bars stripping the waxy layer and lightly bruising the thick stems.

MAKE: TAARUP (Denmark)   MODEL: 305, 306, 307

The Danish company Taarup specializes in grassland machinery and its disc cutting system allows cutting rates of up to 9 miles per hour. The 305 has 5 discs and a 2.0 m cutting width, the 306 has 6 discs and 2.4 m width, and the 307 has 7 discs and 2.76 m width. The 307 with 'auto swather' can dump out swath to left or right.

MAKE: NIEMEYER (West Germany)
MODEL: RO 187

Niemeyer manufactures a wide range of mowers and mower conditioners including front and rear mounted models. The RO 187 has a cutting width of 1.85 m and a minimum power requirement of 45 hp. It has 3 blades per disc and weighs 675 kg. The conditioner unit consists of a horizontal rotor fitted with spring tines.

MAKE: KRONE (West Germany)   MODEL: AM Series

Krone disc mowers are available with working widths of 1.65 m, 2 m and 2.40 m. They are simply constructed for ease of maintenance and smooth operation. A mower is attached to the tractor by a 3-point fixing and it can be hydraulically lifted to a vertical position for transporting. Models AM 201 and 241 can be fitted with a conditioner.

MAKE: DEUTZ-FAHR (West Germany)
MODEL: SM Range

Deutz-Fahr offers conventional rear mounted machines with working widths from 1.65 m to 2.60 m, and front-mounted mowers up to the same width. The latter when used with a rear mounted machine give a 5 m wide cut with a single pass. Or, a loader can be mounted at the rear to save two operations.

MAKE: AGRIMECH (UK)   MODEL: Grasshopper

The Agrimech Grasshopper is a heavy duty, high capacity mower designed for contractors, dehydrators and large acreage grass farmers. The 3 m cut produces a swath to match the capacity of the big forage harvesters and, with the high speeds possible, can give an output of up to 10 acres an hour. An optional conditioner fits to the rear.

MAKE: WESSEX (UK)   MODEL: P18 Rotary Mower

The P18 is a robust and versatile rotary cutter designed to work in a variety of conditions with tractors from 30 to 50 hp. Two main versions are available; a professional model, the P18/W with full castoring rear wheels, and the P18/S, a skid mounted version suitable for rough applications like verges and paddock topping plus orchards and stud farms.

MAKE: BAMFORD (UK)   MODEL: C160 Mower

The finger bar mower has been designed for the smaller acreage grass farmer who requires a quality mower at modest cost. It is strong and simple and attaches to almost any tractor. The 1·5 m finger bar is pivoted to allow it to follow any irregularities of the ground and it can be hinged up for transport.

MAKE: FERRARI (Italy)   MODEL: Type 702

This Italian firm of agricultural manufacturers produces a range of finger bar type mowers. The Type 702 is fitted with either a petrol or diesel engine of 13–14 hp, drum brakes, 4 forward and 2 reverse gears and a PTO for operating implements. The cutter bar, 1.10 m wide, is fitted with closely spaced guards.

Rotary rakes

MAKE: NIEMEYER (West Germany)
MODEL: Rotary Tedder

After the grass or alfalfa is cut and laid in windrows, the tedder spreads it out and aerates it for drying. Niemeyer makes several versions to suit different mower swaths with from 2 to 6 rotors. When working at reduced rpm the tedder can also make loose windrows to minimize the absorption of dew at night.

MAKE: NIEMEYER (West Germany)
MODEL: Rotary Rake

The Niemeyer rotary hay rakes are available as front or rear mounted machines and will work equally well in hay, straw or freshly cut grass. The single and twin machines will make single or double windrows or simply turn them over. The crop is picked up gently and laid into fluffy, aerated and straight windrows.

Balers

MAKE: JOHN DEERE (USA)
MODEL: 550 Round Baler

The 550 Round Baler can roll up everything from short, dry brittle straw to long, damp silage hay and bale it with minimum effort. The operator can choose a bale diameter from 1 m to 1.8 m and bale formation is automatically stopped at the required size. The electronic bale monitor assists in forming even rolls.

MAKE: CLAAS (West Germany)   MODEL: Rollant 44

The Claas Rollant range of round balers is manufactured in 4 sizes from 0.90 m to 1.8 m. The 44, for instance, produces a bale of 1.2 m diameter and 1.22 m width. The operation is completed by a series of driven rollers around the perimeter of the baling chamber. Bales can be automatically wrapped in either twine or net.

MAKE: WELGER (West Germany)   MODEL: RP12

The German firm of Welger are baler specialists and claim to have invented the system that many other companies now use. The RP12 has been specifically developed to handle grass crops for round bale silage but can also work with hay and straw. A variable density control allows the operator to select the density of the bale required.

MAKE: MASSEY FERGUSON (Multi-national)
MODEL: Round Balers

The Massey Ferguson Round Balers, of which there are 3, have closely spaced tines for good even pick-up and the open throat in the forming chamber assists bale starting. The bale density is controlled by hydraulic pressure and heavy duty springs giving a hard core and tighter bale.

MAKE: VICON (Holland)   MODEL: RP 1250

The Vicon RP 1250 produces round bales 1.20 m wide and from 0.6 m to 1.5 m in diameter as required, making it well suited to any crop. It is fitted with a bale size indicator and automatic pick-up shut-off. A combination of wide and narrow belts grow with the bale as it is formed.

MAKE: VICON (Holland)   MODEL: SP 471

The SP 471 square baler is a heavy duty baler more suited to the larger farm. The auger is fed by closely spaced tines on the pick-up and presents pre-compressed material to the packer fingers through a wide feed opening. Grooved bales are formed in the long bale chamber and tied with Deering-type knotters.

MAKE: VICON (Holland)   MODEL: HP 1600

The Vicon HP1600 is a high density baler. It produces large, highly compressed bales tied on the short side with four galvanized wires. The HP1600 has a capacity of 45–50 bales per hour and given a normal yield of 8–12 bales per acre, the harvesting capacity is therefore 5 to 7 acres per hour. A typical silage bale weighs 550 kgs.

MAKE: JOHN DEERE (USA)   MODEL: 342A Baler

The 342A is a rugged, high capacity machine with 6 pick-up bars and teeth spaced just 6.1 cm apart. The adjustable compressor bar matches crop and condition, starting the pre-compaction the moment the hay leaves the ground. The material is then moved by auger sideways into a large specially shaped feed opening.

MAKE: WELGER (West Germany)   MODEL: AP 73

The Welger AP 73 is designed for cereal farmers who operate large combine harvesters and who, therefore, need high output balers with wide pick-ups to speedily clear big swaths and contractors who bale a variety of different crops to re-sell. The Welger has been developed to produce accurately shaped and densely compacted bales.

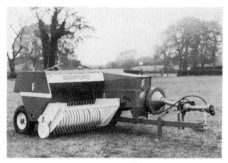

MAKE: BAMFORD (UK)   MODEL: BX 7

A positive gear and shaft drive to the major driven units of this baler are claimed as distinct advantages giving a more efficient, reliable and better engineered machine. It is robustly built and can operate over long periods. The 1.62 m wide pick-up is fed by a twin fork cross-feed system with 3 tines on each of the feed and packer forks.

Forage harvesters

MAKE: CLAAS (West Germany)   MODEL: Jaguar 85

The Jaguar 85 has been designed for the larger farmer and agricultural contractors and to make use of the higher power output of the larger tractors. It can be fitted with a quick-attach 1.97 m wide grass pick-up or a 3-row maize attachment to handle row widths of 65–85 cm. Three lower rollers convey the crop and 2 upper ones straighten and compress it.

MAKE: JOHN DEERE (USA)
MODEL: 3760 Forage Harvester

The 3760 suits tractors from 70 to 120 hp and it has

several features which save PTO power. One of these is the Dura Drum cutterhead which has 24 segmented knives mounted around a drum type base. This also works like a paddle to eject material through the spout without an additional fan. The pick-up is 1.57 m wide.

MAKE: TAARUP (Denmark)   MODEL: 106

The Taarup 106 precision chop forage harvester is a trailed machine suitable for middle range tractors of 45–80 PTO hp. Chop lengths can be varied from 7.5 mm up to 40 mm, and control of the discharge chute is carried out from the cab. Articulated rollers ensure even feed and flywheel and PTO speeds can be altered by changing pulleys.

MAKE: KRONE (West Germany)
MODEL: Short Chop Silage Wagon HSL 2502

The Krone HSL 2502 is a combined harvester and trailer. The cutting drum with dual stars, arranged in a spiral, conveys the harvesting material in a continuous movement from the pick-up to the 41 fixed blades. The 35 mm cut forage is then moved by means of a moving floor to the rear of the trailer.

MAKE: FIATAGRI (Italy)   MODEL: Hesston 7700

The Hesston 7700 is a self-propelled forage harvester powered by 200 hp, Fiat 8 litre, turbo-charged engine. Chopping length is variable from 33 to 132 mm and cutting is carried out by 8 helicoidal knives. Transmission is by a Laverda 3-speed rear axle and hydrostatic variable speed. The spout can rotate through 270 degrees.

HANDLING AND FARM VEHICLES

Through the ages farming has been transformed from a most labour intensive activity to one where almost every job can now be performed by a machine. Many of these machines are of course expensive and some can only be afforded or justified by the larger farms, which we have seen a trend towards in the last decade or two. The sophistication and cost of modern farm machinery has given rise to the emergence of specialist agricultural contractors, who are hired to carry out particular tasks as and when required, rather than the farmer having money tied up in expensive machinery that lies idle for part or most of the year.

One of the big changes in recent years has been the introduction of specialist handling equipment to compete with the traditional tractor and further to extend the role of the farm 'workhorse'. These machines specialize in lifting and moving around the farm such matter as silage, grain or modern bagged fertilizers. One farm materials handler can move a pallet load of sacks to where they are required in minutes, as opposed to the traditional method of several men spending several hours in hard manual labour. This, of course, saves money and frees the men to concentrate on more demanding tasks.

Finally, we take a look at some of the many specialist farm vehicles and trailers available throughout the world for particular jobs. They range from the massive lorry-type tractor units to the small Continental vehicles for use in mountain terrain. There are specialist machines (for carrying loads such as spraying equipment) which are designed to minimize compaction and thereby help the farmer in his struggle to maintain the quality of his land. We look at vehicles that are equally at home on the farm or the road and we examine a variety of small machines which have amazing cross-country ability and are gaining in popularity on the farm. They save the farmer walking even to the most difficult areas to reach and, perhaps, carry vital supplies of food in harsh conditions. We conclude with a small but interesting selection of trailers.

Handlers and loaders

MAKE: SANDERSON (UK)   MODEL: Teleporter 2

The British Sanderson Teleporter 2 is a rugged farm materials handler with an operating capacity of 2.25 tonnes and a lift height of 5.59 m with 2.62 m maximum forward reach. The 4-wheel steering gives impressive manoeuvrability and the 4-wheel drive through equal sized wheels fitted with high flotation tyres ensures excellent traction. The 86 hp water cooled direct injection diesel engine drives through a 4-speed synchromesh gearbox and both axles have limited slip differentials. Full power hydrostatic steering is applied via twin rams for each wheel and there is a selector for crab steer and front wheel steer only, for road use. The cab is fully glazed and sound proofed with an overhead guard.

156

MAKE: SANDERSON (UK)
MODEL: The SB Series Forklifts

For those who prefer the traditional forklift layout, Sanderson manufactures a range known as the SB Series. These rough terrain forklifts are available with 2- or 4-wheel drive with lifting capacities from 2000 kg to 5000 kg. Manual or torque convertor transmission is available on most models and 2 engines are offered giving 64 hp or 86 hp. Differential locks are fitted as standard and the rear axle on the 4-wheel drive models has a limited slip differential. The Sanderson has low friction Duplex and Triplex I-beam roller masts, with extra clear view giving a lift height of 6.7 m. A large range of attachments is also available.

MAKE: JCB (UK)   MODEL: Loadall

The vehicles in the JCB range of telescopic materials handlers are known as Loadalls and are claimed to be the world's best selling forward reach rough terrain materials handlers. There is a choice of 6 telescopic and 2 monoboom models with either 2- or 4-wheel drive. The JCB 520-4 and JCB 520-4HL are known as Farm Specials and are equipped for handling on the farm. They are powered by a turbocharged 89 hp Perkins diesel and have large radial flotation tyres and the JCB safety cab. The Farm Specials have a hydraulic tow hitch, auxiliary trailer hydraulics, 5-spool valve block, pallet fork, chaff guard, propshaft guard and roof screen wash/wipe.

MAKE: JCB (UK)   MODEL: 412 Farm Master

The 412 Farm Master is for all-round materials handling on the farm. It is powered by a turbocharged 4-cylinder engine which develops 89 hp and drives all 4 wheels although there is an optional 2-wheel drive disconnect for better road travel. The transmission with large capacity torque convertor and 6 forward and 6 reverse gears incorporates full power shift modulation for on-the-move gear changes and faster cycle times. The British built Farm Master is articulated to maintain 4-wheel ground contact at all times. Attachments include general purpose buckets; potato, grain and root crop buckets, muck forks and a bale grab.

MAKE: CLIMAX (UK)   MODEL: Tough Terrain

The British Climax company, formerly Coventry Climax, has been making forklift trucks since 1946. The latest Tough Terrain is a robust masted truck available with a lifting capacity of either 2.5 or 3.0 tonnes and 2- or 4-wheel drive. It is powered by a 3860 cc direct injection Perkins engine which produces 76 hp. Drive is taken care of by a 4-speed forward and reverse torque convertor transmission with a heavy duty axle with torque proportioning differentials. Full power hydrostatic steering gives finger tip control and it is claimed that the masted truck is more straight forward in operation than the boom type.

MAKE: CATERPILLAR (USA)   MODEL: Cat 910

The Cat 910 agricultural all-wheel drive loader from Caterpillar is powered by a 5.2 litre direct injection diesel which produces 65 hp at the flywheel. The transmission gives full on-the-move gear shifting without deceleration and the torque convertor adjusts speed to the load and job. Steering is articulated at the centre point.

MAKE AND MODEL: Multi-loader (UK)

The Multi-loader is a compact materials handler for use in low buildings, through narrow doors or in any area where space is restricted. It has 4-wheel drive and 4-wheel steering. Without its canopy it can clear a 1·8 m lintel and turn in 4.6 m between walls. It is powered by a 26 hp Kubota diesel.

MAKE: SAMBRON (UK)   MODEL: J24T

The Sambron J24T is a telescopic boom machine with a reach of 3.45 m and a maximum lift capacity of

1200 kg at full reach. It is powered by a Perkins 72 hp engine and has hydrostatic transmission with slow approach pedal and instant forward/reverse. It is fitted with an integral quick release attachment system.

MAKE: MATBRO (UK)   MODEL: Teleram

The Teleram was designed for farm materials handling. It can be fitted with a variety of forks, buckets and specialized attachments and used for silage making, silage feeding, mucking out sheds and yards, loading, spreading, cleaning slurry lagoons, grain loading, etc. It is powered by a 91 hp Ford engine, has centre pivot steering and oscillating rear axle for stability.

MAKE: RWC (UK)   MODEL: Teleshift

The Teleshift TS240, 2-wheel drive, and TS440, 4-wheel drive, models are said to be the only central cab telescopic twin boom materials handlers on the market. The cab being central rather than offset gives good all-round visibility and booms on either side of the cab give strength without excess weight. The British designed and built Teleshift is compact to work in restricted space yet can place 2-tonne pallets 5 m high. It is powered by a Ford 86 hp engine driving a torque convertor with 4-speed transmission and power shift forward/reverse and fast hydraulics. A bucket attachment can be changed to a fork in 25 seconds.

MAKE: RWC (UK)   MODEL: Minishift

The Minishift was designed for farmers as a budget priced go-anywhere loader that can handle silage, muck, fertilizers and other farm jobs. It has a 4-wheel drive hydrostatic transmission and infinitely variable ratio forward and reverse but is cheaper than a medium-sized tractor and front end loader. Power is by a 45 hp Perkins unit.

MAKE: CASE (Multi-national)
MODEL: 1835B Uni-loader

The Case Uni-loaders are designed to carry out jobs normally done manually. Hydrostatic transmission gives all wheel traction and independent drive to each side. They can therefore turn 360 degrees within their own length and can manoeuvre around obstacles, pass down narrow isles and through low openings. They are powered by a Case 36 hp 2694 cc engine.

MAKE: CASE (Multi-national)
MODEL: 1845B Uni-loader

The Uni-loader 1845B is similar to the 1835B but a little larger. It is powered by a slightly more powerful engine and like its smaller brother has chain drive to all wheels. With safety in mind, both models have a seat belt, strong cab frame, protective grilles and automatic braking. All controls are by levers, leaving the feet free to assist balance. With its various attachments which include a backhoe, the Uni-loader is claimed to be a forklift, tree stumper, post-hole borer, yard cleaner, refuse handler, snow clearer, landscaper, trencher and, of course, a loader.

MAKE: CLARK BOBCAT (Multi-national)
MODEL: Bobcat Range

The Bobcat, claimed to be the original compact skid loader, is available in 10 sizes. All models have 4-wheel drive with hydrostatic transmission and the ability to turn 360 degrees in their own length. The rated capacities range from the 315 at 270 kg to the 943 at 1089 kg. They are extremely compact and capable of working in low, narrow and confined spaces eliminating costly manual labour and tiresome time-consuming tasks. The 540 shown here has a tipping capacity of 726 kg and an operating capacity of half that weight. The larger 642, also shown, has a tipping capacity of 1000 kg.

MAKE: CLARK BOBCAT (Multi-national)
MODEL: 300 Farm Boy

The 300 Farm Boy was designed specifically to meet agricultural requirements. The range of attachments includes buckets, backhoes, grapples, muck forks, angle booms, landscape rakes and earth augers. These implements allow this Bobcat to clean, handle manure, fertilizer, feed and silage, to dig trenches, post-holes, backfill and landscape. It is driven by a 12.5 hp Kubota petrol engine.

MAKE: KELLVE (Sweden)
MODEL: 6-20 Front Loader

The Swedish Kellve company manufactures a range of front end loaders for attaching to tractors. The 6-20 is a high lift type with a telescopic lift arm and can be raised to a height of nearly 5 m. The loader is connected to the tractor's ordinary hydraulic system and can be fitted in just a few minutes.

MAKE: TANCO (UK)   MODEL: 978 Front Loader

Tanco manufactures a range of front loaders and a very wide selection of attachments to mate with them. These include a silage grab (as illustrated here), a root fork, a big bale spear, big fertilizer bag jib, big bale gripper, flat 8 bale grab and a bale transporter. There is a 'drive in' system for fitting.

MAKE: BRUFF (UK)   MODEL: BL10 Loader

The BL10 is a short post rugged loader which can be fitted to trucks, tractors, trailers, lime spreaders or cab tops. It is sold throughout the world for work with timber, sugar, compost handling and cotton bale loading. Its performance and high rotating force enable it to load large amounts in rugged and sloping terrain.

MAKE: ECON (UK)   MODEL: Side Unloading Bucket

The Side Unloading Bucket is suitable for handling

salt, aggregate, soil and snow. It is especially useful when working at road sides or alongside trenches and ditches. In each case the tractor drives parallel to the road or trench, without manoeuvring, but using only forward and backward parallel movement. Its load can then be tipped sideways.

MAKE: TAYLOR FOSSE (UK)
MODEL: Round Bale Rollout Feeder

The Taylor Fosse patented Round Bale Rollout Feeder has been specially developed to unwind bales of silage, hay and straw. The bale sits in a cradle and is turned by a spiked conveyor chain running down one side and across the bottom. As the bale turns the feed is delivered over the side.

MAKE: CHILLINGTON (UK)
MODEL: 56 Bale Transporter

The Chillington 56 Bale Transporter is designed for fast pick-up, transporting and unloading of bales. The special Equi-Grip side arms give maximum grip without a centre spear and the extra wide opening gates make it easy to pick-up stacks. The wide axle and flotation tyres give stability with minimum damage to soft ground.

MAKE: WESTMAC TRIOLIET (Holland)
MODEL: Blockcutters

The Blockcutter, made in Holland, cuts, as the name implies, blocks of silage enabling farmers to feed a better quality silage and it cuts cake costs by reducing aerobic deterioration to a minimum. The 'U' shaped frame cuts on all three sides simultaneously with horizontal cutting knives driven by hydraulic cylinders.

MAKE: TURNER (UK)   MODEL: Snow Thrower

The Snow Thrower is for the farmer who needs a machine quickly available for clearing after a heavy fall of snow without having expensive specialist equipment lying idle for long periods. It can either be 3-point linkage mounted, PTO driven or attached to a tractor's front-end loader and driven hydraulically.

Farm vehicles

MAKE: VOLVO BM (Sweden)   MODEL: 5350 TC

The Volvo contractor's chassis combines the advantages of a rough terrain vehicle with the flexibility of interchangeable bodies for maximum utilization. To combat difficult conditions it has low ground pressure, 4-wheel drive with diff-locks all round and articulated steering. Equipment can be fitted for soil injection, fertilizer distribution, muck or lime spreading and transporting bulk crops.

MAKE: VOLVO BM (Sweden)   MODEL: 5350 B 6 × 6

The large rugged Volvo chassis is also available in 6-wheel drive form for long haulage runs both on and off the road. It is powered by a 6731 cc turbocharged diesel producing 213 hp. The rear terrain bogie has independent axle suspension to give each pair of wheels individual movement with good ground contact.

MAKE: TURNER (UK)   MODEL: Ranger Tug

The Ranger Tug as the name implies is used for towing wheeled machinery around and features 4-wheel steering for extra manoeuvrability. The permanent 4-wheel drive gives greater towing power and all wheels are independently sprung. The low centre of gravity gives good stability and the forward control cab good visibility.

MAKE: DORSET DESIGN AND BUILD (UK)
MODEL: G.P. Series

The G.P. Series of vehicles were designed for general purpose operation where ground damage is undesirable and flexibility of operation is required. All models feature 4-wheel drive and 4-wheel steering to give good traction and manoeuvrability. The GP4, 5 and 6 are fitted with a forward raked screen cab, and the GP8 and GP9 have a traditional rearward sloping screen. They are powered by Deutz direct injection air cooled engines, the GP8 being a 4-cylinder and the GP9 a 5-cylinder. Transmission is hydrostatic giving stepless gear selection. A typical application is as a self-propelled crop sprayer combining the advantages of fairly low ground pressure and a good clearance over the crop.

MAKE: EUROPLUME (UK) MODEL: Hauler

The British manufactured Hauler is a very versatile all-terrain vehicle. It tips, tows, seats 2 people and carries a payload of 800 lbs. The farmer can mount a fertilizer spreader, sprayer or stock cage quickly and easily on its rear platform. The sides can be dropped to turn the Hauler into a flat bed for carrying wide and bulky loads. Fitted with low ground pressure tyres, it can tackle difficult terrain and wet or soft ground. The Hauler has an inbuilt tow bar allowing the operator to tow, for example, loads, mowers or harrows. It is powered by a 17 hp 2-cylinder Kohler engine with a transaxle and integral differential, making it a very useful small workhorse on the farm.

MAKE: LAND ROVER (UK) MODEL: Ninety

Land Rovers are famed throughout the world for the

multiplicity of their applications in some of the worst conditions found. The Ninety is as sturdy as previous models but has improved performance, comfort and agility. Its durability is ensured by its aluminium body. It has permanent 4-wheel drive with a lockable centre differential. Coil spring suspension gives good traction, handling and ride. The Ninety is available with 2.3 litre petrol, 2.5 litre diesel or 3.5 litre V8 petrol engines, all coupled to a dual range 5-speed transmission. Body styles include County, Station Wagon, Hard-top, Soft-top and Pick-up.

MAKE: LAND ROVER (UK)   MODEL: Range Rover

The famous Range Rover defies definition. It is an estate car and a luxury car but also can be, and is, used as a working all-terrain vehicle. Its 3.5 litre lightweight, all aluminium V8 engine drives through permanent 4-wheel drive with high and low range gears, and a differential lock when required. The self-levelling suspension make it an excellent tow vehicle with a capability of pulling 4 tonnes. It can carry 5 people in comfort and with the rear seat lowered has 71 cubic feet of load space. The Range Rover has power steering and the option of 2 or 4 doors.

MAKE: CORNTON ENGINEERING (UK)
MODEL: Gopher

The Gopher is powered by a 340 cc 4-stroke 11 hp Honda engine and drives through a variable speed torque converter with forward and reverse geared transaxle with combined differential. The chassis is made from welded box section steel and the body is fibre glass. Steering is rack and pinion and the fuel tank has a capacity of 6 litres which gives 3 to 4 hours running. It has a top speed of 20 mph and can be registered for road use. Low pressure tyres ensure that no damage is done to the terrain, and the low centre of gravity and pivoting beam front axle make it safe even on steep slopes. The Gopher can be used for transporting feeding blocks to the sheep on the hill or spraying, mowing, etc.

MAKE: VEE PEE (France)   MODEL: Vee Pee 8

The remarkable Vee Pee 8 is an 8-wheel drive vehicle which offers a useful payload capacity of personnel or equipment, and the ability to cross terrain other vehicles cannot cope with. It is amphibious and has a very low ground pressure thanks to its 8 wheels and balloon type tyres which spread the load and thus avoid damaging ground compaction. It has tremendous traction and the ability to climb 45 degree gradients easily and safely. Fitted with the optional tracks, snow and estuary mud of any depth can be travelled over. The '8' has seating for 6 or can carry 540 kg of equipment. It has a 34 hp engine and a top speed of 23 mph. Among its uses are sheep feeding, carrying essential supplies and rescuing stranded climbers.

MAKE: VEE PEE (France)   MODEL: Vee Pee Truck

The Vee Pee Truck can carry a useful payload or

specialist equipment over the most difficult terrain including swamps and bogs. Fitted with the optional PTO and full hydraulic system, the Vee Pee Truck can operate a tipping body, tower platform, welding plant, etc., thus enabling vital maintenance work to be carried out in normally inaccessible places. The Truck can also be fitted with a full van-type body to make a good cross country workshop or a 10-seater personnel carrier. It features 8-wheel drive, a 34 hp petrol or 50 hp diesel engine and can carry crop spraying and fertilizer applicators irrespective of weather conditions.

MAKE: HONDA (Japan)   MODEL: ATC 200 Big Red

The Honda 200 is a 3-wheel all-terrain vehicle with a number of uses on the farm. It is rugged but comfortable and is fitted with a high-torque 13 hp 200 cc engine with a 5-speed, dual ratio gearbox providing good towing ability. The '200' is fitted with a drive shaft rather than chains.

MAKE: MERCEDES BENZ (West Germany)
MODEL: Unimog U1000

The Unimog U1000 is an all purpose vehicle which can be used for carrying loads including spraying equipment and can even plough with a 4-furrow reversible plough. Its 4-stroke 5675 cc diesel produces 95 hp, enabling the U1000 to achieve 50 mph on the road. It has 4 equally sized wheels and 4-wheel drive with differential locks on both axles and air brakes. The fully synchromesh gearbox has 16 forward and 16 reverse gears and full hydraulics and PTO are offered. The versatile Unimog can push, pull and carry which enables it to double as a tractor and general all-round farm vehicle.

MAKE: CAMISA (Italy)   MODEL: HP40

The Camisa is manufactured in Italy and has a 4-stroke air-cooled 40 hp 2-cylinder diesel engine. It has 16 gears, split 8 forward, 8 reverse, and 4-wheel drive. Unusually it has a tri-lateral hydraulic tipping device allowing the rear platform to tip rearwards or to either side. A PTO is optional.

MAKE: PGS (Italy)   MODEL: 3000 & 4500

The PGS is a basic chassis and running gear which will take a whole host of implements and accessories as required. Typical uses are muck spreading, transporting hay in bulk, spraying and spreading, mowing and even ploughing. It can also be fitted with a multi-level platform for fruit pickers.

MAKE: VEE PEE (France)   MODEL: Mule

The Mule has been developed to compete with the Japanese 3- and 4-wheeled 'trikes'. It features 6 driven wheels for excellent cross country ability and stability on gradients up to 45 degrees. It has a full roll cage and seating for 2. The carrying ruck has a payload of 150 kg and the machine will pull 700 kg. It has the engine and transmission from the Citroen Visa which gives 34 hp. Weather protection with the full windscreen, roof covering and optional doors are advantages of the Mule and snow tracks can be supplied.

MAKE: VEE PEE (France)   MODEL: Bison

The Bison is a cross between a tractor and an all-terrain vehicle. It is designed to satisfy the requirement for a lightweight low ground pressure machine with a good cross-country ability which will lift and operate tractor mounted equipment. It is a 6-wheeled machine powered by a Renault diesel engine of 2068 cc derated to 60 hp for longevity. Hydrostatic transmission is used giving an infinitely variable speed range up to 15 mph. Turning the Bison is achieved by varying the hydraulic flow to the drive motor on each side of the vehicle. The extremely manoeuvrable machine is ideal for cross country use and operating in plantations or on difficult gradients. This type of transmission reduces the 'scrub' produced by skid steering machines. Three point linkage and PTOs can be front or rear mounted.

MAKE: SCHILTER (Switzerland)
MODEL: 1300 Transporter

The Swiss made Schilter is a small vehicle with a number of uses on Alpine farms. It can be fitted with a number of implements such as a spraying tank, or forage harvester. It is powered by a 2-cylinder MWM Dieselmotor and it is seen here involved in forestry work with snow chains fitted.

MAKE: BUCHER (Switzerland)
MODEL: Granit 2400 & 2800

These are small multi-purpose transporters fitted with Kubota water-cooled diesel engines producing 36 and 42 hp respectively. They have all-wheel drive, front and rear differential locks and a PTO. The Bucher can be fitted with a rotary tedder, muck spreader, a green and dried forage loader and a loading platform for haulage.

MAKE: SCHILTER (Switzerland)   MODEL: LT

LT signifies load tractor and sums up the multi-purpose role of the Perkins 40 hp 4-cylinder engined machine. It has a 5 ratio gearbox and 4-wheel drive with a payload of 2.5 tonnes and top speed of 15 mph. The example shown has a front-mounted automatic loading device and can have various interchangeable bodies.

MAKE: EVENPRODUCTS (UK)
MODEL: Growmobile

Designed by growers for growers, the Growmobile is a mechanical tool carrier which is lightweight, has complete visibility and can carry a large range of implements individually or in unison. It can take a 6-seeder unit, two 3-gang granule units, front fertilizer applicator, rear spray boom and slug bait unit simultaneously, thus completing 5 jobs in one pass.

Trailers

MAKE: COLLINS (UK)   MODEL: 6 Tonne Twin Axle

The Collins 6 Tonne Twin Axle trailer is very strongly built with a central backbone box section chassis, the box section having a far greater resistance to twist and buckle than a channel iron chassis. Split tailboards or hydraulically lifted tailboards are available and the rear lighting is well protected.

**MAKE: FORTSCHRITT (East Germany)
MODEL: TO88**

This special trailer is capable of carrying 10 tonnes

of agricultural bulk material such as silage, chopped and non-chopped dried forage and manure. Using the optional D353 manure spreader, rotten manure may be uniformly distributed over a width of 6.5 m. A scraper belt feeds the manure to the 4 vertical spreading drums. When using the F997 body for heavy goods, chopped dried forage and silage can be easily transported and distributed in uniform swaths. With the hydraulically operated rear panel, harvested crops may be dumped from the rear in between 2 and 20 minutes as required without being driven over. It is seen here being towed by a 4-cylinder, 110 hp, 6560 cc ZT tractor manufactured in East Germany under licence from MAN of West Germany.

MAKE: WEST (UK)   MODEL: Trailer Range

The West trailers are of monocoque construction with a parallel chassis and tapered body. They are produced in 5, 6·5, 7, 8 and 10 tonne capacities and they have heavy duty axle beams. Extras include front/side loading silage sides, up and over rear door and a grain shute.

MAKE: WEST (UK)   MODEL: Hi-Feeder

The West Hi-Feeder feeds virtually all foodstuffs including chopped silage, forage maize, brewers' grains,
hay, chopped kale, beet tops and a variety of green
crops. It can feed either from within or over a 1.37 m
high feed fence and has a capacity of approximately 4
tonnes. Feed discharge is controlled entirely from the
driving seat.

MAKE: TURNER (UK)   MODEL: Mutti

The Turner Mutti complete diet feeder was intro-
duced to the British market in 1977. Each of the three
models—6, 9 and 11.5 cubic metres—is equipped

with continuous spiral augers developed to handle lush grass type silage. A dense mix is given which reduces secondary fermentation and the feed is distributed through an hydraulically adjustable discharge gate and elevator.

MAKE: NEWBERN (UK)   MODEL: Power Frame

The Power Frame provides an auxiliary PTO allowing the farmer to use, when towed by a tractor, 2 implements in tandem. It can be towed behind a 100 hp tractor and converts the tractor into the equivalent of a 220 hp power plant. It has a Category II 3-point linkage and a Ford 122 hp 6200 cc engine.

INDEX

FARM MACHINERY